D1719053

THE REBEL
PUBLISHING
HOUSE

▨ Editors: Swami Yoga Pratap Bharati and Ma Yoga Sudha
▨ Design and Typesetting: Ma Deva Harito
▨ Production: Ma Deva Harito
▨ Printing: Thomson Press (India) Limited
▨ Published by The Rebel Publishing House Pvt. Ltd.,
   50 Koregaon Park, 411 001 Pune MS, India
▨ Copyright: Osho International Foundation
▨ Second Printing, Revised Edition
▨ All rights reserved.
ISBN 81-7261-018-1

120 Letters

written by Osho to a beloved

disciple, Ma Anandmayee.

In a meditation camp in

Mt. Abu, Rajasthan, India,

Osho announced that she

had also been His mother in

a previous incarnation.

$\mathcal{S}$eeds of
WISDOM

"Having sown the seed, I leave.
You see to it that the seed does not remain only a seed."

OSHO

I TOO AM a farmer. I had sown some seeds and they have sprouted ...and now they have flowered. My whole life is filled with the fragrance of these flowers, and because of this fragrance, I am now in a different world. This fragrance has given me a new birth, and now I am no longer that which can be seen by ordinary eyes.

The unseen and the unknown have flung open their closed doors, and I am seeing a world which is not seen through the eyes, and I am hearing a music which ears are not capable of hearing. What I have found and known is wanting to flow, just as the mountain waterfalls and springs flow and rush towards the ocean.

Remember, when the clouds are full of water they *have* to shower. And when the flowers are filled with fragrance they *have* to give off their fragrance freely to the winds. And when a lamp is lit, the light is bound to radiate from it.

Something like this has happened in me, and the winds are carrying away from me the seeds of inner revolution. I have no idea in what fields they will land and who will tend them. I only know that it is from seeds like these that I have attained the flowers of life, of immortality, of the divine. And in whatever field they land, the very soil there will become the flowers of immortality.

In death is hidden the immortal and in death is life, even as flowers are hidden in the soil. But the potential of the soil can never become realized in the absence of seeds. The seeds make manifest that which was unmanifest and give expression to that which was latent.

Whatever I have, whatever I am, I want to give away as seeds of wisdom, of divine consciousness. What is attained through *knowing*, love gives away in abundance. In knowledge one knows of God; in love one *becomes* God. Knowing is the spiritual discipline, love is the fulfillment.

Osho

मेरे किया,

योग/ अनुभव गहराएँगे।
बस ध्यान करें।
ज्ञान रूके।
संकल्प रूके।
तभी की ओर उतारा गया गलत __शब्द__ भी अर्थ नहीं आता है।
इसलिए, यही शब्द का तो अर्थ ही नहीं है।
चलो और देखो।
अभी जो __बुद्धि__ है।
ज्ञान अवस्था नहीं।
अर्थ तो अनुभव है।
ज्ञान विश्वास नहीं।

1 RENUNCIATION AS SUCH DOES NOT EXIST

I HAD BEEN TO A VILLAGE. I heard someone there saying: "Religion lies in renunciation, and renunciation is an arduous and demanding discipline."

As I heard this, I was reminded of an incident from my early childhood. I had accompanied a picnic party to the bank of a river. The river was small but with a vast expanse of sand. On the sandy bank there lay many pebbles in luminous colors. I felt I had stumbled on a treasure. By the evening I had collected so many pebbles that it was not possible to bring them home with me. Tears came into my eyes when I had to leave them behind as I left, and I was surprised to see my companions' lack of interest in those pebbles.

That day they seemed to me to be great renouncers. When I think of it today, I see that there is no question of renunciation once you have known stones as stones.

Ignorance is indulgence.

Knowing is renunciation.

Renunciation is not a doing; it is not something to be done, it just happens. It is a natural result of knowing. Indulgence is mechanical: that too is not a doing – it is a natural result of ignorance.

Hence, the idea that renunciation is a hard and arduous task is meaningless. In the first place it is not an act – activities alone can be difficult and strenuous – it is an outcome. Secondly, in renunciation what apparently drops is worthless, and what is attained is priceless.

In fact, renunciation as such does not exist, because we gain immensely more than we drop. The reality is that we drop only our bondage, but we gain liberation; we drop only shells but we receive diamonds; we forsake only death but attain immortality; we leave only darkness but attain the light – eternal and infinite.

Where then is the renunciation? Dropping nothing and receiving everything cannot be called renunciation.

2 DEATH IS NEITHER AN ENEMY NOR A FRIEND

LAST NIGHT A MAN BREATHED his last. Today people mourn at his door.

At such moments a memory of an event in my childhood arises in my mind. It was my first visit to the burning *ghats*. The funeral pyre had been lit, and the people were chatting in small groups. The village poet said, "I am not afraid of death. Death is a friend."

Since then I have heard this same assertion in different forms from different people. I have also looked into the eyes of those who say this and have found that these fearless words arise out of fear.

Nothing changes just by giving death beautiful names. In fact, the fear is not of death, the fear is of the unfamiliar. What is unknown creates fear in us. It is necessary to become acquainted with death. This acquaintance brings one to fearlessness. Why? – because it is through acquaintance that one comes to know that there is no death for that which is.

It is only the personality, which we have taken to be our 'I', that shatters, that dies. It shatters because it is not. It is only a composite, a joining of a few elements. As this disintegrates, the personality shatters. This is what death is. Hence, as long as personality is taken to be one and the same as the true self, there is death.

Move deeper from the personality, and as you arrive at the true self, deathlessness is attained.

The path of this journey, the penetration from the surface of personality to the core of the self, is religion.

It is in samadhi, enlightenment, that acquaintance with death happens. Just as darkness ceases to exist the moment the sun rises, so death ceases to exist when samadhi is attained.

Death is neither an enemy nor a friend, it simply does not exist. One needs neither to fear it nor not fear it, one has only to know it. Ignorance of it is fear, knowing it is fearlessness.

3 EMPTY THE MIND AND IT IS THERE

ONE DAY I WENT to a temple. The crowd there was engaged in worshipping the deity. The devotees were bowing down before the idols. An elderly man who had come with me said, "Nowadays people do not have faith in religion. So very few people visit the temples."

I said, "Where is the religion in a temple?" What a self-deceiver man is! He deceives himself by taking as God the idol created by his own hands. He satisfies himself by taking the scriptures – the product of his own mind – as truth.

Whatsoever is the creation of man's own hands and mind is not religion. The idols sitting in the temples are not images of God but of man himself. And what is written in the scriptures is but a reflection of man's own desires and thinking, not the truth seen within. It is not possible to express the truth in words.

It is not possible to have an idol of truth, because truth is boundless, infinite and formless. It has no form, no name, no attribute. The moment it is given a form it disappears. In order to attain it, all idols and all physical conceptions have to be dropped; the whole cobweb of self-fabricated fallacies has to be swept away.

That uncreated truth reveals itself only when man's consciousness is liberated from the prison which his own mind has created.

In fact, rather than building temples in order to reach the truth we should demolish them; instead of sculpting idols we should destroy them. We should drop our obsession with form so that the formless may enter. The moment the manifest leaves our minds, the unmanifest appears. It was there already, but it was hidden beneath the idols and the tangible. Just as we cannot see the empty space in a room stuffed with things – remove those things and the empty space is revealed; it has always been there.

Truth too is like this: empty the mind and it is there.

4 ONLY IN THE SOIL OF FEARLESSNESS...

I HEARD A DISCOURSE this morning. It happened unintentionally. A so-called saint was speaking and I was passing that way when I heard him say, "The way to be religious is to be God-fearing. Only one who fears God is religious. It is fear that brings one to love God. There is no loving without fear. Love is impossible in the absence of fear."

Usually, those who are called religious are religious because of fear. Those who are called moral are also bound to be in fear.

Kant has said, "Even if there is no God, still it is necessary to accept him." Perhaps that is because the fear of God makes people be good.

When I hear such statements, I cannot help laughing. Perhaps nothing else is so mistaken and untrue. Religion has nothing to do with fear. Religion is born out of fearlessness.

It is impossible for love to co-exist with fear. How can fear give birth to love? Out of fear, only the pretense of love can be born. And what else but non-love can exist behind a counterfeit love? Love born out of fear is an impossibility.

Hence, religiousness and morality based on fear are false, not true. They weigh down rather than elevate the energy of the soul. Religion and love cannot be imposed on oneself, they have to be kindled and aroused within.

Truth is not founded on fear. Fear does not support the truth, it is opposed to it. The foundation-stone of truth is fearlessness.

The true flowers of religion and love can be grown only in the soil of fearlessness. Those planted in the soil of fear can only be artificial. The realization of God happens only in fearlessness. Or to put it more correctly, the realization of fearless consciousness is the realization of God.

The moment all fear disappears from the mind, what happens in that moment is the encounter with truth.

5 KNOWING BRINGS VICTORY

THE HEAT OF NOON is at its peak. The flowers on the *palasa* tree are glowing like embers.

I walk along a deserted path. Thick bamboo groves line the path and I find their shade very pleasant.

A familiar bird sings a song, and accepting its invitation I stop there.

A man who is with me asks, "How to conquer anger? How to conquer sex?"

This is a question so frequently asked nowadays. The mistake lies in the question – and I said so to him.

The problem is not to conquer, it is to know. We know neither anger nor sex. This ignorance is what defeats us.

Knowing brings victory. When there is anger, when there is sex, we are not. There is no awareness, hence we are not. What happens in this state of unconsciousness is completely mechanical. When the unconsciousness releases its grip, remorse follows – but that is futile, because the one who now repents will fall asleep again as soon as sex catches hold of him. If he does not sink into sleep – if he lets consciousness, wakefulness and right-remembrance prevail – he will find that there is neither anger nor sex. The mechanicalness is broken and there is nothing to be conquered – the enemy has gone.

You may understand this better through a symbolic story. In the darkness, a rope is taken for a snake. Seeing it, some run away, some get ready to kill it. Both are mistaken, because they both take the rope for a snake. Somebody goes near it and finds that there is no snake at all: he does not need to do anything more than approach it.

Man has only to approach himself. Whatever is within him, he must be familiar with it all. He does not have to fight with anything. And I say unto you that victory comes to him who does not fight.

Right-watchfulness towards one's own mind is the key to victory over life.

6 OUR MIND, TOO, IS FULL OF HOLES

THE NIGHT IS past and the rays of the morning sun are spreading over the fields. We have just crossed a small stream. Hearing the sound of the train, a flock of white herons flies from the white lilies towards the sun.

Then something happens and the train stops. Halting in this

lonely place feels good to me. My unknown fellow passengers are also awake. They boarded at some wayside station in the night. Perhaps taking me for a sannyasin, they come as though to touch my feet. An eagerness to ask something is in their eyes.

Finally one of them speaks: "If it does not inconvenience you, I wish to ask a question. I am interested in God and I have tried hard to reach him, but all to no avail. Does this mean that God does not favor me?"

I say: Yesterday I went to a garden. Some friends were with me. One of them was thirsty so he lowered a bucket into the well. The well was very deep and it took some effort to pull the bucket up, but when it appeared at the top of the well it was empty. All the others laughed.

It seemed to me that the bucket was like man's mind: it had many cracks and holes. Of course, at first it was filled with water, but every drop ran out through the holes. Our mind, too, is full of holes.

Offer the leaking mind to existence as persistently as you wish, it will return to you empty. If you repair the bucket beforehand, my friends, it becomes easy to fill it with water. Of course, the leaking bucket may cause you to undertake many exercises in asceticism, but it will not quench your thirst.

Remember that existence is neither sympathetic nor unsympathetic. It is your responsibility to keep your bucket intact. The well is always ready to offer you water. It will never deny you.

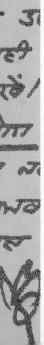

ONE DAY I WAS STANDING on the bank of a river. I saw a paper boat sink in the water.

The day before, some children had built castles of wet sand. They too had tumbled down.

Every day, boats sink and castles tumble.

A woman came to me: her dreams had not been fulfilled, she had lost all interest in life. She had been thinking of committing suicide. Everything seemed futile to her. Her eyes were deeply sunken in their sockets.

I said: Who ever has his dreams fulfilled? All dreams ultimately bring misery because, even if the paper boats sail, how far can they go? The dreams are not in error: dreams are naturally unrealizable. It is we who are at fault: dreaming, we are asleep; sleeping, we can achieve nothing. On waking, we see that we have not attained what we thought we had attained.

Instead of seeing dreams, see the truth. See that which is. This brings liberation, this boat alone is real. This boat alone will carry you to the ultimate fulfillment of your life.

In dreams is death, in truth is life; dreams mean sleep, and truth means wakefulness. Wake up and realize your self. As long as the mind is dreaming, that which sees the dreams cannot itself be seen.

Only the seer is truth. Only the seer is. As soon as we realize this, we can laugh at the sunken boats and fallen castles.

8 "IT IS THOU" IS THE ESSENCE OF ALL RELIGION

T HERE IS A SUFI SONG:

A lover knocked at the door of his beloved. A voice from the inside asked, "Who is there?" The person outside said, "It is I." He heard in reply, "This house has no place for two, 'I' and 'thou'."

The closed door remained closed. The lover retreated into a forest. There he made penance, observed fasts, and offered prayers. After many years, he returned and again knocked on the closed door. Again the voice asked, "Who is there?"

This time the doors were thrown open, for his reply was, "It is thou."

This reply, "It is thou," is the essence of all religion. On the endlessly flowing river of life, 'I' is the only bubble. 'I' alienates the individual from existence. The bubble of 'I' thinks itself distinct from the river, whereas in reality the bubble has no separate existence. It has no separate center, no separate life. It is the ocean, the ocean is its life. Its very existence is in and through the ocean. Even the idea of its being separate from the ocean is ignorance. Look into the bubble and you find the ocean. Look into the 'I' and you find Brahman, the supreme reality.

Where 'I' does not exist, 'thou' too is absent. There is only being. Only existence, pure is-ness, is there. To awaken into this pure existence is nirvana.

9 SEEK THE IMMORTAL LIGHT

THE ONLY LIGHT was coming from an earthenware lamp, but now it too has been blown out. A gust of wind came and extinguished the flame.

How far can we rely on lamps? How long can even a great many flames last when they are so easily blown out? We are surrounded by an ocean of darkness.

A young man is sitting with me. He is very much afraid of the darkness. He says his very being is shaken by it, so much so that he can hardly breathe.

I tell him: Darkness, and darkness alone, envelops this world. And the world has no light that can dispel the darkness. Whatsoever flames there are in the world, sooner or later they themselves die out in the darkness. They come and go, but the darkness remains unaffected. The darkness of the world is eternal, and those who rely on such flames are unintelligent, for these flames are not real. Ultimately they are all overpowered by the darkness.

But there is another world too – a world different from this visible world. If this world is darkness, the other is light. If in this world light is transient and temporary and darkness permanent, in the other one darkness is transient and temporary and light permanent. The wonderful thing is that the world of darkness is far away from us, and the world of light is very near.

Darkness is outside, and light is inside.

And remember, if you do not awaken to the light within, no other light can dispel your fear. Drop your reliance on mortal lamps, and seek the immortal light. This alone can bring you fearlessness, bliss, and the light which no one can take away from you. That alone is ours which cannot be taken away. Only that which does not come from outside is ours.

Of course there is darkness outside your eyes, but look within your eyes to see what is there. If there were darkness there, how could you recognize the darkness? That which recognizes the darkness cannot itself be darkness.

Again, if it aspires to light, how can it be darkness? It is light, hence it aspires to light. It is light, hence it yearns for light. It is light, hence it seeks the light. Light alone can thirst for light. Search for the place from where this thirst arises, make that point your goal, and you will find what you thirst for hidden there.

10 BEYOND POSITIVE AND NEGATIVE

I AM NOT GOD-FEARING. Fear does not take one to God. It is only a complete absence of fear which can take you there.

In no sense am I a believer, either. Belief is blind. How can blindness take one to the ultimate truth?

Nor am I a follower of any religion, because religion cannot be categorized with adjectives. It is one and indivisible.

Yesterday when I said this, someone asked me, "Then are you an atheist?"

I am neither an atheist nor a theist. These distinctions are superficial, merely intellectual. They have absolutely nothing to do with existence. Existence is not divided into 'is' and 'is not': these distinctions are of the mind. Accordingly, both atheism and theism are of the mind, they do not reach the spiritual. The spiritual transcends both positive and negative. That which is, lies beyond positive and negative.

In other words, there they are one, and there is no dividing line between them. No concept accepted by the intellect gains access there. In fact, the theist has to drop his theism and the atheist his atheism: then, possibly, they may enter the world of truth. Both these ideas are the obsessions of intellect. Obsession is an imposition. We are not required to decide what truth is, but only to see it as it is at the moment one opens oneself.

Remember that we do not have to decide about truth, we have to see it. He who drops all intellectual decisions, logical conceptions, mental obsessions and assumptions, in that state of mental innocence, opens himself to the truth – as flowers open themselves to the light. It is in this opening up that seeing becomes possible.

Thus, I call that man religious who is neither a theist nor an atheist. Religiousness is a leap from the notion of many, into oneness.

Where there is no thought, but only absence of thought, where there is no choice, only choicelessness, where there are no words, only wordlessness, there we enter religion.

I WAS OUT for a walk at night. The village road was rugged and uneven. With me was a friend, a monk who had traveled a great deal. There was hardly a place of pilgrimage where he had not been. He sought the path to the divine.

That night he asked me a question: "What is the path which leads to the divine?"

He had put this question to many others. Slowly, slowly, he had become conversant with many paths, but the distance between him and the divine remained the same as ever. It was not that he had not attempted those paths. He had done all he could, but treading the path had been the only result. He had reached no goal, but he was not yet weary of traveling, and his search for new paths continued.

I remained silent for some time. Then I said, "There is no path to attain what I myself am. Paths are for reaching 'the other' and 'the distant'. What is near – not only near, but what I myself am – cannot be attained by means of a path. There is no intervening space for a path. Attainment is of that which is lost – but can the divine ever be lost?"

What can be lost cannot be one's own self.

The self can only be forgotten.

Hence, one does not have to go anywhere: one has only to remember. Nothing is to be done – only known. And to know is to attain. What we need to know is: who am I? To know this is to attain the divine.

One day, when all our efforts seem futile, when no path seems to lead anywhere, then it will become clear that whatever we do will not attain the truth.

No doing will unravel the mystery of the 'I', because all doing leads away.

No doing takes us to existence. Where doing ceases, being reveals itself.

No doing will give that to us, because being is in existence before all activity.

There is no path leading 'there', because there is here.

12 A Matter of Right-Feeling

ONE EVENING THERE WAS a storm on Lake Galilee. A boat was on the verge of sinking; there seemed to be no way of avoiding disaster. Passengers and boatmen were equally helpless. Gusts of

violent wind shook everyone to the core of their being. The waves had begun to break into the boat; the shore was far beyond reach. But amid the raging storm, a man was sleeping soundly in a corner of the boat, unruffled and unworried. His companions woke him up. Shadows of imminent death lurked in their eyes.

Waking, the man asked, "Why are you all so frightened?" – as if there were no reason at all to be afraid. His companions stood dumbfounded. They could not utter a word. He asked them again, "Have you no faith?"

On saying this, with calmness and courage he rose and walked slowly to the side of the boat. The storm was lashing and raging in its final attempt to overturn the boat. Addressing the turbulent lake he said, "Peace. Be still."

He said, "Be still," as though the storm were a naughty child.

The passengers must have wondered what kind of madness this was. Do storms pay heed to entreaties? But even as they watched, the storm subsided and the lake became as calm as if nothing had happened.

The man had been heard.

The man was Jesus Christ and the incident is two thousand years old. But it seems to me that these events happen every day.

Are we not constantly in the midst of a storm, a restlessness? Is not the shadow of imminent death constantly in our eyes? Is not the inner lake of our minds continuously disturbed? Does not the boat of our lives constantly seem to be on the verge of sinking?

So is it not proper that we ask ourselves, "Why are you so afraid?" and "Have you no faith?" Should we not go into ourselves and say to the turbulent lake within, "Peace. Be still?"

I have tested this and found that the storms do subside. It is simply a matter of beginning to feel at peace, and peace descends. We make ourselves restless; we can also make ourselves calm. The attainment of peace is not a matter of practice, it is a matter of right-feeling.

Peace is our nature. Even in the midst of deep restlessness, there is a center where we are at peace. There is a person within us who is calmly asleep in the midst of all our storms. In this peaceful, still, unworried spot is our real existence. The miracle is that, despite its existence, we become restless. There is no miracle in returning there.

If you wish to be at peace, you can be so right now, right here. Practice brings results in the future, right-feeling brings results instantly. Right-feeling is the only real transformation.

I USED TO ASK MYSELF, "Who am I?" It is impossible to count how many days and nights I passed in this query. The intellect gave answers heard from others, or born of conditioning. All of them were borrowed, lifeless. They brought no contentment. They resonated a little at the surface, and then disappeared. The inner being was not touched by them: no echo of them was heard in the depths. There were many answers to the question, but none were correct, and I was untouched by them. They could not rise to the level of the question.

Then I saw that the question came from the center, but the replies touched only the periphery. The question was mine, but the answers came from outside; the question arose from my innermost being, the replies were imposed from outside. This insight became a revolution. A new dimension was revealed.

The responses of the intellect were meaningless: they had no relevance to the problem. An illusion had shattered, and what a relief it was!

It seemed as if a closed door had been flung open, filling the darkness with light. The intellect had been providing the answers – that was the mistake. Because of these false answers, the real answer could not arise. Some truth was struggling to surface. In the depths of consciousness some seed was seeking the way to break open the ground in order to reach the light. Intellect was the obstruction.

When this became clear, the answers began to subside. Knowledge acquired from outside began to evaporate. The question went ever deeper. I did not do anything, only kept on watching.

Something novel was happening. I was speechless. What was there to do? I was, at the most, simply a witness. The reactions of the periphery were fading, perishing, becoming non-existent. The center now began to resonate more fully.

"Who am I?" – my entire being was throbbing with this thirst.

What a violent storm it was! Every breath quaked and trembled in it.

"Who am I?" – like an arrow, the question pierced through everything and moved within.

I remember – what an acute thirst it was! My very life had turned into thirst. Everything was burning. And like a flame of fire the question stood forth, "Who am I?"

The surprise was that the intellect was completely silent. The incessant flow of thoughts had stopped. What had happened? The periphery was absolutely still. There were no thoughts, no conditionings of the past.

Only I was there – and there was the question too. No, no – I myself was the question.

And then, the explosion. In a moment, everything was transformed.

The question had dropped. The answer had come from some unknown dimension.

Truth is attained through a sudden explosion, not gradually.

It cannot be compelled to appear. It comes.

Emptiness is the solution, not words. Becoming answerless is the answer.

Someone asked yesterday, and someone or other asks every day, "What is the answer?"

I say, "If I mention it, it is meaningless. Its meaning lies in realizing it for oneself."

14 I WISH TO DISTURB THIS SLEEP OF YOURS

I AM NOT A PREACHER. I do not wish to deliver a sermon or a lesson. I have no desire to instill any thought of mine into your mind. All thoughts are futile. Like particles of dust, they cover you up, and then you begin to appear what you are not, and what you do not know appears to be known. This is suicidal.

Ignorance is not dispelled by thought, it is only concealed. In order to awaken knowledge, it is essential to know ignorance in its stark nakedness. For this reason, do not conceal yourself in the garments of thought. Remove all coverings and garments so that you become familiar with your nakedness and hollowness. This will become a bridge to take you beyond ignorance. The acute distress of realizing your ignorance is the starting-point of revolution.

Hence, I wish to expose you, not conceal you. See how many blind faiths, conceptions and fancies you have hidden yourself behind! And you think yourself safe and secure behind these barriers? This is not security but self-deception.

I wish to disturb this sleep of yours. Truth, not dreams, is your sole security.

If you can gain the courage to drop your dreams, you will attain the truth. What a bargain! In order to attain the truth, you have only to drop your dreams, nothing else.

You must break through the unconscious – its thoughts, dreams, fantasies. You must awaken from the seen to that which sees.

The seer alone is the truth; if you attain it, you have attained life.

I said this to someone. Hearing it, he fell into reflection. I told him: You have become engrossed in thought. But that is the slumber from which I urge you to awaken.

A BULLOCK CART IS passing by. I watch its wheels revolving on the axle: the wheels go round and round on what itself is motionless. Motionlessness lies behind all motion. There is inaction behind action. Nothingness dwells within is-ness.

Similarly, one day I saw a violent dust storm. A huge column of dust was rising, circling upwards to the sky, but its center was calm and motionless.

Is not the basic truth of existence revealed in these symbols?

Does not nothingness dwell behind all is-ness?

Is there not inaction behind all action?

Nothingness alone is the center and soul of is-ness. It alone has to be realized. There alone must we be, for that is our real being. We must all become that which, at the center, we already are. We have to go nowhere else other than where we are already.

How is this to be accomplished?

See that which sees and you descend into nothingness. We have to proceed from the seen to the seer. The seen is form, action and is-ness. The seer is formless, inaction, and nothingness. The seen is the other, the ephemeral, the world, bondage, non-liberation, and the cycle of rebirth. The seer is the self, Brahman, liberation, nirvana. See – see him who sees. This is the whole essence of yoga.

This is what I say every day. Or, to put it another way, whatever I am saying contains only this.

16 ASK AND BE QUIET...

THERE IS A THIRST for true knowledge. What a thirst! I see it in everyone. Something is blazing within which wishes to calm itself. And in how many directions man searches for it! Perhaps this search goes on through infinite lifetimes. Seeking some Holy Grail, man's mind keeps on wandering, but at every step he meets nothing but frustration. No path seems to lead there. There is some movement, but no destination ever appears in sight.

Do paths lead nowhere, then?

This question need not be answered. Life itself is the answer. After walking through an infinite number of ways and directions, is not the answer already clear? Is the answer still not received?

In an intellectual reply, the real answer is lost in smoke. When the intellect is quiet, experience speaks out. When thoughts remain silent, wakeful intelligence arises.

In fact, there are no answers to the basic questions of life. Problems are not solved, they are only dissolved. The task is simply to question, and to become empty. The intellect can only ask – it cannot provide the answer. The answer comes only from the void.

The answer comes from the void – knowing this truth, life takes on a new dimension. This state of mind is called samadhi, enlightenment.

Ask and be quiet, utterly quiet, and let the answer come of its own accord. Allow it to come to fruition at its own pace, and in this still state of the mind is seen that which is, that which you are.

The thirst for true knowledge is not quenched without knowing the self. To reach the self, it is necessary to abandon all paths. When the mind is on no path at all, it is in the self. And to know the self is true knowledge. Everything else is only information, because it is indirect. Science is not true knowledge. Science does not know the truth, it only knows the applications of truth. Truth can only be known directly. And any existence which can be known directly is only that of the self.

The moment the mind becomes quiet and still, realizing the futility of search, the doors of the infinite are flung open.

Choiceless consciousness settles in the divine. And the ultimate quenching of the thirst for true knowledge is only in the divine.

17 TOTAL SILENCE IS THE ONLY PRAYER

IT IS PAST MIDNIGHT. I have just returned from a gathering where someone said, "Call the name of the Lord! Remember and repeat his name. If you call him incessantly, he is sure to hear."

I was reminded of Kabir, who said, "Has God become deaf?"

Perhaps Kabir's words have not reached this man.

Then I heard him say, "Ten people are sleeping. Someone calls out, 'Devadata.' It is only Devadata who wakes. The same thing is true of the Lord. Call his name, and he will surely hear you."

Hearing his words I was tempted to laugh. First, it is not the Lord who is sleeping, it is us. He is ever wakeful. It is not he who has to awake, it is us. It is ironic that the sleepers should have to rouse the wakeful!

We should not call him, we should listen for him calling us. This can happen only in silence, only when the mind is completely free of disturbance. When there is no sound in the mind, his resonance is perceived.

Total silence is the only prayer. Prayer is not action; on the contrary, when the mind is doing nothing it is in prayer.

Prayer is not an activity, but a state of being.

Secondly, the Lord has no name, nor has he any form. So there is no means of calling him or remembering him. All names, all forms are imaginary. They are all false. We reach the truth by abandoning names and forms, not by relying on them.

He who dares to abandon everything fulfills the condition for attaining the Lord.

18 THE COURAGE TO SURRENDER ONESELF

I HAVE HEARD:

A fakir was begging. He had grown old, and his eyesight was weak. He stood outside a mosque and called for alms. A passer-by said, "You had better move on. This is not the house of a man who can give you something."

The fakir asked, "Who can be the householder who gives nothing to anyone?"

The passer-by replied, "Madman, don't you know this is a mosque? The owner of this house is the great father, God himself."

The fakir raised his head and looked at the mosque. His heart filled with a burning thirst. A voice within him spoke, "But how can I move from this door? This is the ultimate doorway. Where is the door beyond this?" A strong resolution grew within him. Like an immoveable rock, his heart declared, "I will not leave here empty-handed. Whatever they gain afterwards, those willing to leave here empty-handed have gained nothing."

He sat down near the steps of the mosque. He stretched his empty hands towards the sky. He was thirsty – and thirst itself is prayer.

Days came and went, months rolled by. The summer passed, the rainy season passed, the winter was almost over. Nearly a year had gone. The old man's end was near, but in the last moments of his life, people saw him dancing.

His eyes had an other-worldly glow. His old body radiated light.

Before dying he said to someone, "He who asks, attains. One need only have the courage to surrender oneself."

The courage to surrender oneself.

The courage to annihilate oneself.

The courage to become a void.

He who is willing to disappear attains fulfillment... he who is willing to die achieves life.

EARLY ONE MORNING, Gautama the Buddha was about to speak, but before he could do so, a bird began to sing at the door. In the peace and stillness of the morning, Buddha remained silent. The morning sun went on weaving the patterns of its rays and the bird kept on singing. Buddha was silent; all were silent. In that silence, in that void, the song had become divine. When the song ended the void became even deeper.

Buddha then stood to leave: that day, he uttered no word. That day, the silence itself became the discourse. What he conveyed through that silence could never be conveyed through words.

All that is in this life, in this universe, is wholly divine, is entirely godly. In everything there is the imprint and reflection of the divine. The divine alone is latent in everything; it alone is manifest in everything. All form is divine, all sound is divine. But as we do not remain silent, we cannot hear. And because our eyes are closed, we cannot see. Our minds are too present, and so it is absent.

If we are empty, it is here and it is now.

Truth is, but the self is unconscious – just as there is light but our eyes may be shut. We do not awaken the self, but we search for truth; we do not open our eyes, but we seek the light. Never fall into this mistake.

Drop all seeking, and be silent. Quiet your mind and listen. Keep your eyes open and see. If a fish in the water were to ask my advice in its search for the ocean, what would I say to it? I would say, "Stop searching. Just see: you are already in the ocean."

Everybody is in the ocean. The task is not to find the ocean – it is to start drinking it.

20 SELF-REMEMBRANCE IS THE TRUE PATH

THERE IS A TEMPLE in the neighborhood. Every day, soon after nightfall, they begin to sing and chant hymns and prayers. A strong smell of incense fills the sanctuary. The worship and offerings begin. Musical instruments are played, bells are rung, drums are beaten, gongs are sounded. The priest dances and gradually the devotees too join in.

One day I went to the temple to witness this. What I saw was not worship at all but a kind of stupor. It was self-forgetfulness in the name of prayer. If you forget yourself you forget your sorrow. These forms of religion serve the same purpose as drugs and intoxicants.

Who does not wish to forget the pain of his life? That is why intoxicants were created. That is also why intoxicating rituals were created.

Man has concocted many types of wine, but the most dangerous of wines is not in bottles.

Sorrow is not conquered by forgetting it; its seeds are not destroyed by these methods. Rather, its roots are strengthened.

Sorrow must be conquered, not forgotten. Forgetting it is not religion, but self-deception.

Just as self-oblivion is the way to forget sorrow, self-remembrance is the way to overcome sorrow.

True religion awakens the self completely. All other forms of religion are false. Self-remembrance is the true path, self-forgetfulness leads away from it. Also remember that the 'I' is not quelled by forgetting the self: its hidden current continues to flow. The 'I' disappears only through self-remembrance.

He who knows the 'I' totally can attain to the whole by realizing the disappearance of the 'I'.

The path to the whole is not through forgetfulness of the 'I' but through its disappearance.

It is a fallacy to try to forget the 'I' by remembering God. The way is to annihilate the 'I' by becoming aware of it.

And, when the 'I' ceases to exist, what remains is God.

God is attained by annihilating the 'I', not by forgetting it.

21 MAN'S CONSCIOUSNESS IS LIKE THIS FLAME

SINCE EVENING it has been stormy and rainy. Gusts of wind have lashed the trees. The electric supply has failed, and the city has been plunged into darkness.

In the house, an earthen lamp has been lit, its flame rising up. The lamp is of the earth, but the flame endlessly rises to touch the unknown.

Man's consciousness is like this flame. His body is content with the earth, but there is something else in him which constantly strives to rise above it. This consciousness, this dancing flame, is the life of man. This ceaseless yearning to soar is his soul.

Man is man because he has this flame within him. Without it, he is only clay.

If this flame burns fiercely, a revolution comes into being. If this flame comes to a blaze, the clay itself can be transcended.

Man is a lamp. There is clay in him, but there is light too. If he concerns himself only with the clay, his life is wasted: there must be attention to the light also.

Awareness of light transforms everything because it allows man to see God in the mundane.

THE MORNING IS ended. The sun becomes stronger, and my being wishes to move to the shade.

An elderly schoolteacher is visiting. He has been practicing spiritual disciplines for years. His body is emaciated, skeletal, his eyes dull and sunken. He has been torturing himself, thinking his torture to be spiritual discipline.

The lives of many who are eager to tread the path to the divine are poisoned by this error. For them, attaining the divine takes the form of denying the world, and saving the soul becomes destroying the body. This negativity destroys them, and they cannot see that rejecting the world is not the same thing as realizing God.

The truth is that those who mortify the body actually have faith in the body; those who condemn the world are subtly obsessed with the world. Asceticism binds one to the world no less than hedonism.

True spiritual discipline does not reject the body and the world – it transcends them. And that is achieved by neither indulgence nor suppression. This way is different from both; it is a third way, the way of balance. Balance lies at the midpoint of two extremes, and that which is exactly at the midpoint transcends both polarities.

In fact, it is only by way of illustration that it is called the midpoint: it lies beyond both extremities. To be balanced between indulgence and suppression is not to have a little indulgence and a little suppression: it is to have neither. It is not a compromise, it is a balance. At the extreme is imbalance, at the midpoint is balance. At the extreme is destruction, at the midpoint is life.

To be at the extreme is to perish; both indulgence and suppression destroy life. Imbalance is ignorance, darkness and death.

My spiritual discipline is balance and harmony. When the strings of the *veena* are neither too loose nor too tight, then music arises. Strings which are too loose are as ineffective as those which are too tight. But the strings can be at a point where they are neither too loose nor too tight, and it is this point which gives birth to the melody. This point is the point of balance.

The law of music and the law of balance are identical. Truth is attained through balance.

I mentioned this matter of balance to the schoolteacher, and it seems he paid attention. His eyes bear witness to it: their expression is of someone awakening after sleep. He appears to be peaceful and calm, as if some tension has relaxed and some insight has been attained.

At his departure, I told him, "Drop all your tensions, and then watch. You have dropped enjoyment; drop suppression also. Drop it all, and watch.

"Be natural, and watch. Only by being natural can we become healthy, can we reach the self-nature."

By way of reply, he said, "What now remains to be dropped? It is already dropped. I am returning peaceful and free of burden, as if a nightmare has ended. I am very grateful." His eyes had become very innocent and calm, and his smile was sweet. Though old, he seemed like a child.

I wish these things could be clear to everyone who seeks God.

23 LEAVE THE MIND ALONE AND WATCH

IF YOU WISH to attain truth, then drop the mind. As the mind ceases to exist, truth is revealed, in just the same way as opening the doors allows the sunlight to enter. Like a wall, the mind prevents the truth from entering, and the bricks of the wall consist of thoughts. Thoughts, thoughts and more thoughts…this chain of thought constitutes the mind. The sage Ramana Maharshi once said to someone, "Stop your thoughts, and then tell me where the mind is."

Where there is no thought, there is no mind. If there are no bricks, how can there be a wall?

A hermit came last night. He asked, "What shall I do with the mind?"

I said, "Do not do anything with it. Leave the mind alone and watch. Leave it completely alone and go on watching. Just as one watches the flow of the water while sitting on the bank of a river, go on watching the flow of your thoughts. Do not identify yourself with them, do not attach yourself to them. Just go on watching, just be alert. By your watching, your thoughts will vanish and your mind will disappear."

And, as the mind disappears, what is experienced in its vacant place is the soul, is the truth, because that alone is.

24 SO THAT THE FORMLESS SKY MAY BE ATTAINED

ONE DARK, COLD NIGHT, a monk was staying in a temple. In order to ward off the cold he had burned a wooden statue of the temple deity, but sensing the blazing fire the priest awoke.

When he saw the statue burning he was stunned. Overcome with anger he could not utter a word, so unthinkable was the act. Then he noticed that the monk was searching for something in the heap of ashes. The priest asked him, "Whatever are you doing now?" The monk replied, "I am searching for the bones of the deity's body." At this, the madness of the monk became clear to the priest. He said to the monk, "Madman, how can there be bones in a wooden statue?" The monk replied, "Then please do me the favor of bringing another statue. The night is long and very cold."

When I think of this story, it appears to me that I myself am that mad hermit.

If only we were free of images so that we could see the imageless! If we persist with the form, we cannot reach the formless. With our eyes fixed on the form, how can we leap into the ocean of the formless? Can someone who worships something outside himself return into himself? Throw the non-essential, manifest, to the flames so that only the essential, unmanifest, remains. Let the massed clouds of form be scattered, so that the formless sky may be attained. Let the form melt, so that the boat may reach the ocean of the formless. He who launches his boat from the shore of the finite certainly reaches the infinite and becomes one with it.

25 PRAYER IS SOMETHING WE ARE

WHAT IS PRAYER? Is it self-forgetfulness? No, it is not self-forgetfulness. All forgetting, drowning and losing oneself is only a form of intoxication. Techniques such as these are not prayer but an escape. It is possible to lose oneself in words, in melody, to lose that which is, in the hypnosis of music and dance. This forgetting and losing oneself may even be pleasurable, but it is not prayer, it is unconsciousness.

Prayer, however, is conscious awareness.

Is prayer an activity? Is doing something a form of prayer?

No, prayer is not an activity but a state of consciousness. Prayer is not something we do, it is something we are. Its essence is inactivity. When all activity ceases, and only a witnessing consciousness remains, that is prayer. The word prayer implies activity, and the word meditation also implies activity; but both these words should be used, not for doing...but rather for a state of consciousness. To be in nothingness, in silence, in wordlessness – this is prayer, this is meditation.

I mentioned this yesterday in a prayer assembly.

Someone asked me later, "Then what shall we do?"

I said: For a while, do nothing. Move into complete relaxation. Let both your body and your mind become quiet. Silently, watch the mind. By itself, it becomes calm and empty. It is in this emptiness that we come close to the truth. It is in this emptiness that that which is, both within and without, manifests itself. Then within and without disappear and pure existence remains. The totality of this pure existence is called God.

26 EMPTINESS ITSELF WAS THE GROUND

EVENING HAS MERGED into night. Some people have come. They say, "You teach nothingness, but the thought of nothingness terrifies us. Is there nothing we can hold on to?"

I tell them that courage is certainly essential for a leap into nothingness. But in fact, those who jump in do not attain nothingness, they attain wholeness. And those who hold on to something achieve nothing. Can an imaginary handhold really help you?

It is only through emptiness that we can attain truth. And in emptiness there can be nothing to cling to.

I tell them a story:

One dark, moonless night, a traveler passing through unfamiliar mountains slipped and fell into a deep chasm. Catching hold of a bush, he hung suspended. There was darkness all around. Below him was also impenetrable darkness and the dreadful abyss.

For many hours he clung to the bush, and throughout this time he suffered the pangs of imminent death. It was a winter night and gradually his hands became cold and numb. Soon he would have to release his grip, and then he would fall into the abyss. No effort could save him, and already he saw himself in the jaws of death.

He fell – but nothing happened. There was no abyss at all. The moment he let go, he found himself standing on the ground just a few inches below.

This has been my experience also. Falling into emptiness, I discovered that emptiness itself was the ground. By dropping the support of the mind, we attain the support of the divine.

The courage to jump into nothingness is man's only true courage, and those who cannot summon up the strength to enter nothingness remain unfulfilled.

I WAS RETURNING HOME from a morning walk. On the bank of a river I came across a small spring. Sweeping dry leaves from its path, the stream was racing towards the river. I saw its headlong rush and its blissful merging with the river. Then I saw that the river too was in haste.

And then I perceived that everything was hurrying – to meet the ocean, to be lost in the infinite, to achieve completeness, fulfillment, brushing aside the dry, dead leaves from its path.

The drop of water longs to merge with the ocean. This longing is fundamental to life. All our striving arises from this yearning, and to fulfill it brings true joy. To be finite is to have sorrow, to be incomplete is to have sorrow. It is because of being finite, being incomplete, that life ends in death. In their absence, life is immortal. Because of them, it is shattered into pieces. In their absence, it becomes an undivided whole.

But man halts as the small drop of the ego, and there he becomes severed from the endless flow of life. Thus, abandoning the sunlight, of his own free will, he tries in vain to find fulfillment in the feeble flame of an earthen lamp. But he cannot find contentment, because how can a drop be content to remain only a drop? There is no answer other than becoming the ocean. For the drop, the ocean is the goal – it has to become the ocean. It is essential for the drop to disappear. It is essential to destroy the ego. When the ego becomes Brahman, then alone is fulfillment possible.

It is only the fulfillment of being the ocean which establishes one in truth. And it is this fulfillment alone which liberates, for how can he who is not fulfilled become liberated?

Jesus Christ has said: "He who tries to save his life loses it, and he who loses it attains it."

Let me say the same. This alone is love. Losing oneself is love. Accepting death in love is the way to attain the life of the divine.

This is why I say, "Drops, hurry towards the ocean! The ocean alone is your destination. Gladly accept death in love, for that alone is life. To halt before reaching the ocean is to perish, but to reach the ocean is to transcend death."

IT HAPPENED: The disciple of a sage passed away. The sage went to the disciple's house where the dead body was lying and people were crying. The sage approached and asked in a loud voice, "Is this man dead or alive?"

This astonished and puzzled the mourners. Why was the question asked? The dead body lay there – was any further evidence needed?

For a while there was silence, and then someone asked the sage, "Please, sir, can you answer your own question?"

Do you know what the sage replied? He said, "That which was dead has died. That which was alive still lives. It is only the link between the two which has given way."

Life does not die, and death does not live.

Those who do not know life call death the end of life. But birth is not the beginning of life, nor is death its end. Life exists within birth and death, and beyond them also. It exists before birth and it lives after death. Birth and death exist within life, but life itself is not born, nor does it die.

I have just returned from a cremation. As the funeral pyre blazed, people said, "It is all over."

I said, "You have no eyes, and so that is the way it appears to you."

29 THE STORMS OF DUALITY

I HAVE RETURNED from a journey to a place where I met many *sadhus* and *sadhvis*. *Sadhus* are everywhere, but there is no *sadhana* – meditation – in their lives. They are as plentiful and as false as artificial flowers.

Without meditation, religiousness is impossible. What now goes by the name of religion only strengthens irreligion. On the surface we have religion, but inside there is only irreligion.

And this is only natural. You can push plants without roots into the soil, and they will make a beautiful party decoration, but will they grow fruits and flowers?

The roots of religiousness lie in meditation, in yoga. Without yoga, the life of a seeker can only be either pretense or suppression. Neither is of any use.

To pretend good conduct is hypocritical. And suppression too is fatal. Both involve effort and struggle, but achieve nothing. What is suppressed does not die: it simply moves down into deeper layers of the being.

At one extreme there are the pangs of sensual enjoyment, the heat and fever of a life scorched in its own flames, and the endless race to quench an unquenchable thirst. At the other extreme we find the burning flames of suppression and self-torture. Escaping the well of one extreme, we fall into the deep ditch of the other.

Yoga is neither indulgence nor suppression. It is awakening from both. Both extremes of this duality should be avoided. We cannot transcend a duality by choosing only one of its sides. He who chooses and clings to either of the sides gets himself caught and enslaved by it.

Yoga is not a clinging to anything – it is dropping all clinging. It is not leaving off one thing only to take up something else. Remain aloof, drop all clinging. It is the clinging itself which is the mistake. It is this that leads one to fall into the well or the ditch. It is this that leads one to extremes, into dualities, into conflicts, while the right path is where there is no extreme, no duality, no struggle.

Do not make choices; instead, move into the consciousness which chooses. Do not fall into duality; instead, move into the state of knowing which perceives the duality. This movement is true wisdom, and it is this wisdom which is the door to light.

That door is near. And those who liberate the flame of their consciousness from the storms of duality attain the key which opens this door to truth.

30 THIS EMPTINESS THAT THE OCEAN ENTERS

I SEE PEOPLE WITH such crowded lives that I feel pity for them. There is not even a fraction of space, of empty sky within them. And how can anyone be liberated who has no sky in him? For liberation, what is needed is sky inside, not sky outside. He who has sky inside is at one with the sky outside. And when the inner sky becomes one with the universal sky, that merger, that mingling, that transformation is called liberation. And that is the realization of God.

Hence, I never urge anyone to fill himself with God – rather, I say that you should empty yourself, and then you will find that God has filled you up.

During the rains, when the clouds pour forth water, the hills remain dry, but the valleys, which had also been dry, are filled. Be like the valleys, not like the hills. Do not fill yourself, empty yourself. The divine is constantly showering on you: he who is empty to receive that shower becomes full.

The value of a pitcher is precisely that it is empty. The more empty it is, the more the ocean can fill it.

A man is also worthy to the extent that he is empty. It is this emptiness that the ocean enters and makes full.

WHEN I SEE spiritual seekers, I find that they are all engaged in disciplining their minds. But truth cannot be attained by disciplining the mind. On the contrary, it is the mind which is the obstacle in realizing the truth. You should drop the mind, not control it. Drop the mind and you find the door. Religion is attained neither in the mind nor through the mind. It is attained in the state of no-mind.

Mah Tzu was a seeker. Living in a solitary hut in the hermitage of his master, he tried day and night to discipline his mind. Even if someone came to visit him, he ignored them.

One day his master visited Mah Tzu's hut. Mah Tzu ignored him also, but his master remained there all day, rubbing a brick against a rock. Finally, unable to endure this any longer, Mah Tzu asked, "What are you doing, sir?" His master replied, "I have to make a mirror of this brick."

Mah Tzu said, "A mirror from the brick? Have you gone mad? Even if you rub the brick for the rest of your life, it will never become a mirror." On hearing this, his master began to laugh and asked Mah Tzu, "And what are you doing? If a brick cannot become a mirror, can the mind become one?"

In fact, neither the mind nor the brick can become a mirror. The mind actually is the dust which has covered the mirror. Drop it, put it aside; then alone can you realize truth. The mind is a mass of thoughts, dust particles which have to be swept away. What is left when they are swept away is eternally spotless consciousness. In that no-mind state, free from thoughts, we see the eternal truth which had been hidden behind a smoke-screen of thoughts.

If there is no smoke of thoughts, the smokeless flame of consciousness alone remains. That is what has to be attained; that is what one has to be. That is the fulfillment of your seeking.

32 THIS UNCHANGING ONE

FIRST THE MORNING, then the noontime came and departed. Now the sun is setting: a beautiful sunset is spreading over the western horizon.

Every day I see the sunrise, the burgeoning of the day and its passing. And I also see that I do not rise, or pass into afternoon or sunset.

When I returned from travel yesterday, I perceived this. Travel always brings the same insight: the path changes, but not the traveler. Travel itself is a change, but the traveler appears unchanging.

Where was I yesterday and where am I today? What was I then and what am I now?

But what I was yesterday, I am today too. What I was then, I still am. The body is not the same, the mind is not the same, but I am the same.

In space and time there is change, but there is no change in 'I'.

Everything is a flowing current, but this 'I' is not a part of it. The 'I' is not with the current, but outside it and beyond it.

This eternal traveler, ever-new, ever-familiar, is the soul. In the changing universe, to awaken to this unchanging one is liberation.

33 WHO IS THIS CONSCIOUSNESS?

I SEE YOU AND also what lies beyond you. Sight which stops with the body does not see. How transparent the body is! No matter how solid, it fails completely to conceal what lies beyond it.

But if there are no eyes to see, then everything changes. Even the sun ceases to exist. The whole game is of the eyes. We do not realize the light through thinking and logic.

There is no alternative to the authentic eye; it is essential. To see the spiritual we need an inner eye, we need insight. With it, everything is visible to us. Without it, we are blind both to the light and to the divine.

The one who wants to realize the existence of others beyond the body has first to look beyond his own mortal existence. Only to the extent one looks within is the other revealed. The entire insentient world becomes filled with consciousness only to the extent to which my own consciousness is developed. The world is only what I am myself. The day I realize the totality of my consciousness, the world no longer remains a mere world.

Self-ignorance is the world; self-knowledge is liberation.

Each day, I say to everyone, "Can you not see who resides within you? who inhabits this body of bones and flesh? who is imprisoned within your outward appearance?"

What immensity is present within this insignificant body!

Who is this consciousness? What is this consciousness?

Without inquiring into this, without comprehending this, life has no meaning. Even if I understand everything but do not understand myself, then that understanding is valueless.

The energy which can apprehend the other, can also apprehend the self. How can it not?

It is simply a question of changing direction. From that which is seen, we have to move to that which is seeing. The change of attention from the seen to the seer is the key to self-realization.

From the flow of thoughts, awaken to that which witnesses them. And a revolution takes place. Like a great spring of pure water suddenly bursting forth, the current of consciousness sweeps away all unawareness from life.

34 WE HAVE TO GIVE MAN BACK HIS ROOTS

UNTIL LAST EVENING, this plant was alive. Its roots were in the ground and there was life in its leaves. It was green and lustrous. Swaying in the breeze, it shed bliss all round. I had passed by it many times and had felt the melody of its life.

Yesterday someone disturbed it, loosening its roots, and coming to it today I found that the plant had breathed its last. This is what happens when the roots are dislodged from the ground. Everything depends on the roots. They are invisible, but they hold the whole secret of life.

Plants have roots; man also has roots. Plants have a ground; man also has one. When the roots are dislodged from the ground, plants dry up; so too with man.

I was reading a book by Albert Camus. The opening sentence of the book ran, "Suicide is the only significant problem for philosophy." Why? – because nowadays man finds no purpose in life. Everything has become meaningless and futile.

What has happened is that our roots have been shaken. We have lost our link with the source of life, without which, life is nothing more than a meaningless story.

We have to give man back his roots. We have to give him back his ground. Those roots are the soul, that ground is religion. If this can be done, flowers can bloom once again in humanity.

35 ALL HOUSES ARE HOUSES OF CARDS

I WAS INVITED into a family's home and returned only after dusk. A beautiful incident took place at the house. There were many children there and they had built a house with a pack of playing cards, which they took me to see. It was beautiful, and I praised it. But the lady of the house said, "What is there to praise in a house of cards? The gentlest breeze will topple it to the ground."

I began to laugh, and the children asked why. But even as we spoke, the house of cards collapsed. The children became sad, and the lady of the house said, "You see!"

I replied, "Yes, I saw. I have seen other fine houses too, and they all collapse just like this one."

Even palaces of stone are but houses of cards – palaces built by old men just the same as those built by children. We all build palaces – palaces of fantasy and dreams. And then a gentle breeze tumbles them to the ground. In this sense we are all children. Maturity is a rare phenomenon, and most people die still children.

All houses are houses of cards. Realization of this makes an individual mature. Even then he continues to build them, but by then it is only acting.

To know that being in the world is only acting, is to become free of the world.

Only that which we attain with this understanding will not be destroyed by the first gust of wind.

36 SANNYAS IS NOT FORCED, IT IS FOUND

L AST NIGHT IT RAINED. It is humid and just now it has begun to drizzle again. Moist winds are driving the falling leaves as far as the door. It seems as if the autumn is here, preparing for the arrival of spring. The pathways are covered by dry leaves which make a sweet rustling sound when one walks on them.

I have been watching those leaves for a long time. That which becomes ripe falls. Though leaves fall continuously from dawn to dusk, it causes the trees no pain. This demonstrates a wonderful rule of life: to pluck the unripe fruit brings pain, but the ripe fruit falls by itself.

A sannyasin has come. Renunciation has not yet become blissful for him: rather, it is painful and difficult. Taking sannyas did not come to him naturally, he stretched out for it. The leaves of attachment, ignorance, possession and ego were still unripe. He has applied force: the leaves have fallen, but their falling has caused pain. This pain prevents peace from coming. I think I should go this evening and tell him the secret of the falling leaves.

Understanding, not renunciation, comes first. When sannyas comes through understanding, the world falls away like dry leaves. Sannyas is not forced, it is found.

After the revolution of understanding, renunciation becomes a pleasure, not a pain.

THERE IS A DIFFERENCE between knowledge and knowing. One is the amassing of information, simply an intellectual understanding; and the other is a knowledge which is experience, knowing, a living realization. One is the accumulation of dead facts, the other is the understanding of living truth. There is a great difference between the two – the difference between earth and sky, darkness and light.

In fact, intellectual knowledge is not knowledge at all: it is the illusion of knowledge. Can a blind man know the light? This is intellectual knowledge. This illusion of knowledge conceals ignorance, but it is merely a disguise. In the maze of its words and in the smokescreen of its thoughts, ignorance is forgotten.

But to forget ignorance is more deadly than ignorance itself. Where ignorance is visible, there comes a desire to rise above it. Where ignorance is invisible, it is impossible to free oneself from it.

The so-called wise men are destroyed in their ignorance.

Knowledge – the true knowledge – does not come from outside. Be aware that what comes from outside is not knowledge, it is information. Be careful not to fall into the illusion of knowledge, for whatever comes from the outside forms an additional layer over the self.

Knowledge awakens from within. It does not come, it awakens. And for this to take place we have to peel away the layers covering the self, not add to them.

Knowledge is not acquired, it is discovered. Acquired knowledge is information, discovered knowledge is experience. Life has to be forced to fit the shape of acquired knowledge. But the fit cannot be exact, and so a conflict arises between that knowledge and life.

Our behavior naturally shapes itself to conform with discovered knowledge; it is impossible to run counter to true knowledge. Such a thing has not yet happened on this earth.

I am reminded of a story. Two sages were traveling along the hazardous paths of a thick forest. Their relationship was that of father and son. The son was in front and the father behind. The path was lonely and frightening. Suddenly they heard the roar of a lion. The father said to the son, "Hide behind me, there is danger ahead." The son laughed and continued to walk in the lead. Again his father warned him. Suddenly, the lion was facing them. Death was imminent. The son said, "Since I am not the body, where is the danger? Isn't this what you always preach?" The father ran away, shouting, "Mad boy, keep away from the lion!" but the son continued to walk ahead, laughing.

The lion pounced on him. Already he had fallen, but he saw clearly that that which had fallen was not 'I'. He was not the body, and so he could not die. Now he understood what his father used to say. And the difference is immense. His father was sad, the tears welling up in his eyes; but the son had remained a witness, in life as in death. He had no misery, no pain. He remained unmoved and unattached, because whatever was happening to his body was happening outside. He himself was not involved in any way.

This is why I insist that there is a difference between knowledge and knowing.

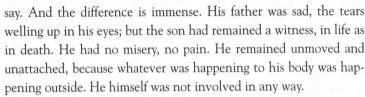

38 AWAKENING INTO THOUGHTLESSNESS

WHAT IS SAMADHI?

Someone has said, "The mingling of the drop with the ocean."

Someone else has said, "The descent of the ocean into the drop."

But I say: It is the disappearance of both the drop and the ocean. Samadhi is where there is neither the drop nor the ocean. Samadhi is where there is neither one nor many. Samadhi is where there is neither the finite nor the infinite.

Samadhi is oneness with existence.

Samadhi is truth, samadhi is consciousness, samadhi is bliss.

'I' is not present in samadhi. Samadhi is what remains when 'I' ceases to exist.

And perhaps this 'I' which is not 'I' is the real 'I'.

'I' has two existences: the ego and the Brahman. I am not the ego, but I seem to be. I am the Brahman, but I seem not to be.

Consciousness, pure consciousness is Brahman.

I am pure witnessing consciousness, but because I identify with the stream of my thoughts, I do not see this. Thought itself is not consciousness. Consciousness comprehends thought. Consciousness is the witness of thought. Thought is the object and consciousness is the subject. To identify the subject with the object is to be unconscious. This is the opposite of samadhi. This is sleep.

What remains in the absence of thought is consciousness. To be in what remains is samadhi.

Awakening into thoughtlessness opens the door to existence. Existence means that which is. Awaken into it: this is the essence of the message of all the enlightened ones.

I SEE THE GARDENER sowing seeds. He then puts manure in the soil, waters it and waits for the flowers to blossom. Flowers cannot be compelled to bloom. They need patience.

Love and patience.

The seeds of the divine should be sown in the same way. And similarly, we need patience to await the blooming of the flowers of the divine life.

Prayer and patience – to resist this, to be impatient, leads nowhere. Impatience does not foster growth.

If one waits peacefully, patiently and lovingly, one fine morning the flowers bloom and their fragrance fills the courtyard of one's life.

To attain the flowers of the infinite, infinite patience is essential. But remember that if you are prepared for so much patience, your attainment can come in an instant.

Infinite patience is the only condition for realizing the infinite. The moment this condition is fulfilled...the attainment. After all, it does not come from outside, it grows from within. It is already present, but because of our impatience and restlessness we are unable to see it.

40 JUST SITTING ON THE BANK

M AN'S MIND IS WONDERFUL. It holds the mystery of the world as well as of liberation. Sin and virtue, bondage and liberation, hell and heaven, all abide within it. Darkness and light both belong to it. Birth is in it and death too is in it. It alone is the door to the external world, it alone is the ladder to the internal being. With its disappearance we transcend both. The mind is everything. Every-thing is its play, its own imaginative creation. If it disappears, all imagining ceases to exist.

Yesterday, I said this somewhere. Someone came forward to ask, "The mind is very unstable and fickle. How to drop it? The mind is polluted. How can it be made pure?"

Then I told a story.

After Buddha had become old, one afternoon, he stopped to rest at the foot of a tree in the forest. He felt thirsty, and Ananda went to a nearby mountain stream to fetch water. But just a few minutes before, some carts had crossed the stream and the water had turned muddy. Rotting leaves and scum had begun to float on the surface. Ananda returned without water and said to Buddha, "The water in the stream is not clean; I shall go back to the river and bring water from there." The river was very far off, and Buddha asked him to fetch water from the stream. After a short while Ananda returned again empty-handed: the water did not appear to him to be fit to drink.

But Buddha made him go back once more. On the third occasion, when Ananda reached the stream, he was amazed. The stream had now become completely clear and unpolluted. The mud had settled and the water had become pure.

I find the story very interesting. The state of the human mind is just the same. The traffic of life comes and stirs it up, but if one goes on watching it, sitting in silence and patience, the impurities settle and a natural clarity returns. In this clarity of mind, life renews itself. It is only a matter of patience, silently waiting, and without doing anything the impurities of the mind settle.

One has only to become a witness and the mind becomes pure. Our task is not to make it pure. All difficulty arises because of doing. Simply watch it, just sitting on the bank – then see what happens!

41 SING YOUR LIFE'S SONG

IN THE STILLNESS of the night someone is playing on a flute. The moonlight appears to have frozen. This cold, solitary night, and the notes of the flute coming from far away sweet as a dream – all this is unbelievably beautiful.

How much nectar can a hollow bamboo shower!

Life too is like a flute – empty and void in itself, but at the same time having a limitless capacity for melodious notes. But all depends on the player.

Life becomes what one makes of it; it is one's own creation. It is merely an opportunity. What type of song one wants to sing is entirely one's own decision. This is the dignity of man, that he is free to sing songs of both heaven and hell.

Everyone can create divine notes on his flute; it is only a matter of practicing a bit with the fingers. A little practice and the attainment is immense. The empire of infinite bliss is attained without doing anything.

I wish to say to each and every heart, "Take up your flute. The time is going fast. See that the opportunity to sing the song does not slip by. Before the curtain falls you have to sing your life's song."

O N THE SPIRITUAL PATH it is essential to know what is the seed and what is the fruit. It is necessary to recognize the beginning and the end. One who moves ahead without recognizing the cause and effect makes mistakes. Just walking is not enough; no one reaches the goal just by walking. The direction and the mode of spiritual endeavor must also be right.

On the spiritual path there is one central thing and there are things which are peripheral also. If the effort is made at the center, the periphery will be taken care of on its own: there is no reason to take care of it separately. It is only the manifestation of the center; it is only the extended center. Hence, efforts on the circumference prove futile. There is a saying, "To beat around the bush." To get involved at the circumference is just like that.

What is the center and what is the periphery?

Knowing is the center and humility the periphery. Knowing is the beginning and humility the outcome. Knowing is the seed, humility is the fruit. But generally people start in the opposite direction: proceeding from humbleness they want to reach knowledge. They want to transform humbleness into knowledge.

But humility cannot be cultivated in ignorance. In fact, humility cannot be cultivated at all. Cultivated humbleness is not humbleness; it is a false covering beneath which the lack of humbleness is suppressed. Practiced humility is a deception.

Darkness is not to be suppressed or concealed: it has to be eliminated. Paper flowers of humility are not to be pasted on to cover non-humility. It has to be eradicated. When it is not there, what comes out is humility.

A forced humility, cultivated in ignorance, is dangerous because in it, what is not appears to be, and thus what has to be brought about vanishes from sight altogether.

In ignorance there is simply no way of bringing about humbleness directly, because the manifestation of ignorance is in itself the absence of humbleness. The lack of humility is nothing but ignorance. A buddha has said, "What can he who is in ignorance do?"

It is not humbleness but knowing that has to be brought about. Knowing itself becomes humbleness.

Knowing illuminates everything: only when it arises do ignorance and illusion disappear. It is only through knowing that infatuation and hatred are eliminated. It is only through knowing that the state of liberation is attained.

I RECEIVED A LETTER in the morning. Someone has asked, "Life is full of misery, yet you talk continuously of bliss? If one looks at what is, all talk of bliss seems to be just fantasy."

Certainly we are surrounded by misery – life is full of it – but that which is surrounded is not misery. As long as we go on looking at that which surrounds us, only misery seems to be there. But the moment we begin to look at that which is surrounded, misery becomes untrue and bliss true.

The whole thing is only a matter of perspective. The seeing which manifests the one who sees is the only seeing. Everything else is blindness. The moment the seer becomes manifest, everything turns into bliss, because bliss is its true nature. The world still remains, but it becomes entirely different. What appeared to be thorns in it because of self-ignorance, no longer appears so.

The existence of misery is not real, because it is shattered by the later experience. Just as the dream becomes unreal on waking up, so does misery after self-realization.

Bliss is truth because it is the self.

44 TO TRANSCEND HUMANNESS

YESTERDAY I GAVE A TALK at a certain place.

I said: I want to make you discontented. That a spiritual thirst, a divine discontent may be born in all – this is my desire. For man to be satisfied with what he is, is death. Man is not the end-point of evolution; he also is only a rung on the ladder of evolution. What is manifest in him is nothing in comparison to what is unmanifest in him. What he is is almost nothing in comparison with what he can be.

Religion wants to awaken everyone from the death of contentment to the life of discontent, because it is only through this discontent that one can reach to the point of real contentment.

Man has to transcend his humanness. It is this transcendence that gives him access to divinity. How will this transcendence take place?

Let one definition be understood, then the process of transcendence is also understood: animality – pre-thinking state; humanity – thinking state; divinity – state beyond thinking. If we go beyond the boundaries of thought, consciousness reaches divinity.

To transcend thought is to transcend humanness.

I SEE GOD IN NATURE itself. I am experiencing him each moment, each minute. Not a single breath passes without meeting him. Wherever my eyes fall, I see he is present. Whatever my ears hear, I find that his melody is being sung.

He is everywhere – it is only a matter of our ability to see. He is, but we need the eyes that can see him. When the eye is ready he manifests himself everywhere, every moment.

At night, when the sky is filled with stars, do not think about them but see them. And when the waves dance on the vast expanse of the ocean, do not think about them but see them. And when a bud is opening into a blossom see it, just see it! When there is no thought but only seeing, a great secret is revealed, and access is gained through the door of nature into that mystery which is God.

Nature is nothing more than a veil over God, and only those who know how to lift that veil become familiar with the truth of life.

A young seeker of truth went to a master. Arriving, he asked, "I want to know truth, I want to know religion. Kindly tell me where to start."

The master said, "Do you hear the sound of the waterfall from the nearby mountain?"

The youth replied, "I hear it clearly."

The master said, "Then start from there, enter from there. There is the door."

Really, the entrance is so near – in the waterfalls descending from the mountains, in the leaves of the trees swaying in the wind, in the sunrays dancing and sparkling on the vast ocean. But there is a curtain at every door and it is not lifted unless we ourselves lift it. In fact, the screen is not on the entrance, but on our vision. Thus a single curtain has covered an infinite number of doors.

46 ONLY IT IS, WE ARE IMAGINARY

THE MOON IS COMING UP. Passing through the trees, its soft light has begun to spread on the pathway. The wind is full of the fragrance of the mango-blossoms.

I have just returned from a symposium. Most of those present there were young people, excited and influenced by modern trends. It is as if no-faith was their only faith and negation the only positive attribute.

One of them said, "I do not accept God. I am free and independent."

This statement reflects only the mood of the time we live in. This whole era is under the shadow of this freedom, without knowing that this freedom is suicidal. Why is it suicidal? – because it is impossible to deny God without denying oneself.

I told them a story:

There was a grapevine spread out in the palace garden of God. It was tired of expanding and expanding, growing and growing, obeying and obeying. It was fed up with dependence, and one day it had the desire to be free. It shouted at the top of its voice so that the whole sky would hear it: "Now I will not grow! I will not grow! I will not grow!"

This rebellion was certainly strange, because it was against the true nature of the grapevine itself.

God looked and said, "Do not grow – what is the need for growth?"

The grapevine was glad; the rebellion had succeeded. It became occupied with efforts not to grow. But the growth did not stop, it never stopped. It busied itself in not growing, and it went on growing and growing. And God knew it beforehand.

This is the situation. God is our true nature; he is our inner law, one cannot go away from it. There is no other way except to be it. However much we may deny it, however much we want to be free of it, there is no liberation from it because it is our very self. In fact, only it is; we are imaginary. This is why I say liberation is not from it, but in it.

47 EVERYONE IS ALONE

A KING HAD IMPRISONED a man of sound health and balanced mind. He wanted to study the effect of aloneness on man. The prisoner continued to shout and scream for some time and to cry and beat his head in his desperation to get out. After all, his entire existence was outside; his whole life was tied up with the other. Within himself he was nothing. To him, to be alone was like not being at all.

Slowly he began to break down. Something within him began to disappear and a quietness overtook him. Crying ceased, tears dried up. His gaze became stony. Even while seeing he would appear to not be seeing.

Days went by, months passed, and finally a year elapsed. All arrangements had been made for his happiness and comfort. What he did not have even while outside was now available to him in the prison. After all, it was royal hospitality!

But by the end of the year, the specialists declared that he had gone mad. Externally he was the same as before, perhaps healthier, but inside? Inside he had already, in a sense, died.

I ask: can aloneness drive a man mad? How can aloneness make one mad? In fact, madness is already there. The outside relationships keep it concealed, aloneness only uncovers it. The restlessness of man to lose himself in a crowd is only to avoid seeing it.

This is why everybody is escaping from himself. But this escape cannot be called healthy. To not see reality is not to be free from it. One who is not healthy and mentally balanced in utter aloneness is in a deception. Sometime or other this self-deception is bound to be shattered. And one will have to know that which is within in its stark nakedness. If this happens unintentionally and suddenly, the personality shatters and goes insane. That which is suppressed sooner or later comes to an explosion.

Religion is the science of descending into this aloneness on one's own. On uncovering layer by layer, an amazing truth is encountered: slowly, slowly, it becomes known that we are really alone. In the depth, at the innermost center, everyone is alone. And it is because of not being familiar with that aloneness that fear is felt.

Ignorance and unfamiliarity cause fear. Once familiarity is there, fear is replaced by fearlessness and bliss. In the realm of aloneness, *satchitananda* – truth, consciousness, bliss – itself is present.

The divine is attained on descending into oneself. Hence I say: Do not run away from aloneness, from yourself, but dive into yourself. Only by diving in the ocean are pearls found.

48 KNOWING IS THE DEATH OF EGO

IT RAINED IN THE NIGHT. The roads are wet, the wind is damp and the sky is overcast with clouds. It seems the sun will not rise. The morning feels very gloomy.

A young man has come. He is well-read and educated – appears to be so. His words smell of books and nothing but books. How boring this smell is!

I listen to him, although he had come to listen to me. He has been speaking for an hour, but whatsoever he has been saying is not his own. This is the kind of mechanical mind that our system of education today is producing. It is not creative. It gives birth to memory, not to the faculty of thinking. Thoughts are gathered, but the ability to think is not attained. This is a fatal situation. Through it, no growth happens to the individuality and the ability to think, to one's capacity for self-experience. The person only repeats other people's words like a machine.

That which only fills the memory system is not real education. Such an education is only an appearance of education. Education must give birth to that insight which is itself capable of looking into the problems. The problems are mine – how can the solutions provided by others help me? And then every problem is so new that no old solution can be a solution for it.

The latent energy within us, the genius, must awaken through education. We should not be stuffed with those thoughts which we have neither lived ourselves nor known ourselves, and which are utterly dead for us and can only increase our burden. Beneath this dead weight the awakening of the genius becomes impossible.

Every day I see such people all around me who are getting crushed under the burden of those ideas which they have not known themselves, but rather accepted from others. The idea that has not been known by oneself inevitably becomes a burden.

Education should not be a passive acceptance of thoughts. Only when education is based on active understanding and creative knowing is it meaningful.

I am forgetting that young man in all these digressions. When he stopped after expressing his thoughts – which are not his at all – he proudly looked around in a gesture that said, "I also know."

How arduous is knowing, but how easy is the ego of knowledge! Knowing is not attained but ego certainly takes over, and remember that the two are polar opposite dimensions. Knowing is the death of ego, and where ego is present it can be inferred that knowing has not happened. It is enough indication of the absence of knowing.

Knowing brings egolessness. The more deeply a person knows, the deeper his realization of knowing nothing. Knowing does not de-mystify existence, it only reveals it. And at that moment, when one is face to face with the whole mystery of the universe and of the self

– at that boiling point the person becomes empty and all his 'I-ness' disappears. Ego was the product of the darkness of ignorance; in the light of knowing it dies.

I kept quiet for a while and then said to him, "I wanted to listen to you but you do not say anything. What you have just said – nothing of it is yours. It is all borrowed, and no richness comes from others' wealth. It may conceal poverty, but it cannot eradicate it."

In the case of truth, only one's own experience is true and alive. If that is there, a revolution takes place in one's life. Otherwise, by carrying the burden of dead, alien thoughts about truth, nothing comes to hand. It only increases the burden, and the possibility of self-realization recedes.

Knowledge that is not one's own becomes a hindrance in the arising of that knowing which can only be one's own.

THE EVENING SEEMS to have come to a standstill. The west-bound sun has long since gone behind the clouds, but the night has not set in yet. There is solitude outside as well as inside. I am alone – there is neither anybody outside nor inside.

At this time I am nowhere, or rather, I am there where there is emptiness. And when the mind is empty it is not.

This mind is amazing. It comes to be experienced like an onion. One day, seeing an onion, I was reminded of this resemblance. I was peeling the onion; I went on peeling layer after layer, and finally nothing remained of it. First thick, rough layers, then soft, smooth layers, and then nothing.

Such is the mind also. You go on peeling off, first gross layers, then subtle layers, and then an emptiness remains. Thoughts, passions and ego, and then nothing at all, just emptiness. It is the uncovering of this emptiness that I call meditation. This emptiness is our true self. That which ultimately remains is the self-form. Call it the self, call it the no-self – words do not mean anything. Where there is no thought, passion or ego, is that which is.

Hume has said, "Whenever I dive into myself, I do not meet any 'I' there. I come across either some thought or some passion or some memory, but never across myself."

This is right – but Hume turns back from the layers only, and that is the mistake. Had he gone a little deeper he would have reached the place where there is nothing to come across, and that is the true self. Where there remains nothing to come across is that which I am. Everything is based in that emptiness. But if somebody turns back from the very surface, no acquaintance with it takes place.

On the surface is the world, at the center is the self. On the surface is everything, at the center is no-thing-ness, the void.

50   WHAT IS THIS 'I'?

I HAVE JUST RETURNED from a walk in the sun. How pleasant the warm sunshine of the winter feels! The sun rose not long ago and the warmth of its rays is gradually increasing.

A man was with me. I was silent all the way, but he kept on talking. As I listened, I noticed how often we use the word 'I'. Everything is tied up with the center of this 'I'. After birth it is probably the awareness of 'I' that arises first of all, and at the time of death it is the last to leave. In between these two points is the expanse of the same 'I'.

How familiar this 'I' is and yet how unknown too! There is no word more mysterious than this in human language. Life passes, but the mystery of 'I' is rarely uncovered.

What is this 'I'? It is not possible to deny it either – even in negation it gets proposed. Even in saying "I am not" it is present. In human realization this 'I' is the most certain, decisive and undoubtable entity.

"I am" – this awareness is there, but who I am is not an inborn knowing. To know that is only possible through spiritual endeavor. All spiritual endeavor is the endeavor to know this 'I'. All religions, all philosophies are answers to this single question.

"Who am I?" – this question is to be asked by everyone of himself. Let everything else drop and this single question remain. Let this quest alone remain resounding in the whole being. Thus this question descends into the unconscious part of the mind.

As the question moves deeper, the superficial identifications start dissolving. It begins to be seen that I am not the body. It begins to be seen that I am not the mind. It begins to be seen that I am that which sees everything – I am the seer, I am the witness. This experience becomes the realization of the true nature of the 'I'. The pure, enlightened, witnessing consciousness is revealed with the arising of this true knowledge. The door to the mystery of life opens.

Becoming acquainted with ourselves, we become acquainted with the whole mystery of the universe. Knowledge of the 'I' becomes the knowledge of godliness.

This is why I say this 'I' is precious. To descend to its ultimate depth is to realize everything.

51 BLISS IS THE TOUCHSTONE OF TRUTH

THE CITY IS ASLEEP in the stillness of the night. I have returned from my walk with a guest. A lot of talking has happened on the way. The guest is a hylotheist and a well-read scholar. He has accumulated lots of arguments. I heard them all in peaceful silence and then asked only one thing: if, through all these thoughts, he was in peace and bliss or not.

At this he felt a little embarrassed and was not able to come up with an answer.

Argument is not a touchstone of truth, nor is thought; only the experience of bliss is the touchstone of truth. If the mindfulness is right, life is filled with bliss-consciousness as a consequence. Mind is there only for the purpose of coming to this point, and the mindfulness that does not bring one here is more of an un-mindfulness.

"Hence," I said to him, "I do not oppose your statements at all; I only request that you put this question to yourself."

Religion is not thought, it is only a science for attaining to divine consciousness. Its test is not in argumentation but in experimentation. It is not an analysis of truth, it is the endeavor for truth and its attainment.

52 THE RECOGNITION OF THE HOST

I AM SITTING IN A HUT. Through the holes in the thatched roof sunlight is falling in circular patches on the floor. Dust particles are visible floating in the beam of the light. They are not part of the light, but they have made the light impure. They cannot even touch the light because they are in every way different and foreign, but because of them the light is seen as impure. The light is still the light, there is no change in its self-nature, but its body – its appearance – has become impure. Because of these foreign bodies the host itself has a different appearance.

A similar thing has happened with the soul of man. There also many particles of dust have become guests, and man's true nature is covered by them. It is as though in the crowd of guests the host is lost beyond recognition – something similar has happened.

But for those who want to know the meaning of life and encounter truth, it is necessary to recognize in the crowd of guests the one who is not a guest, but the host. Without knowing this host, life is just a somnambulism. Wakefulness begins with the recognition of the host. That recognition is self-realization. Through that recognition happens the acquaintance with that which is eternal, pure, buddha-nature.

The light does not become impure because of the dust particles – nor does the soul. The light becomes dull, the soul becomes forgotten.

What kind of dust particles are there on the light of the soul? All that has come into me from the outside is that dust. What is in me other than that is my buddha-nature. All that has been attained and accumulated by the sense-organs is dust.

What is there in me which has not been attained by the sense-organs? Form, taste, smell, touch, sound – apart from these what else is there in me? That which has not been attained by the sense-organs is truth, consciousness. It has not come from the sense-organs, rather it is behind them.

This consciousness alone is my true nature. Everything else is alien, dust. This alone is the host – all the rest are guests. This consciousness alone is to be known and uncovered. Only in this consciousness is attained that wealth which is imperishable.

THE LAST STAR OF THE DAWN is disappearing in the mist. The morning is about to be born, and a rosiness has spread all over the eastern sky.

A friend has just given me the news of the death of some beloved relative; this very night he left his body. After a short silence the friend began to talk on death. He said many things, and then in the end he asked, "Death is an everyday happening, yet everyone lives in such a way as if he will never die. It simply does not enter one's mind that one will also die. How come there is such faith in non-dying amidst so many deaths?"

This faith is very meaningful. It is so because the one who exists in the mortal body is not mortal. The circumference is of death, but at the center there is no death.

The one who is seeing – the seer of the body and the mind – knows that he is separate from the body and the mind. That seer of the mortal is not mortal. He knows, "There is no death for me; death is only a change of the body. I am eternal. Even while passing through death, I, the deathless, remain."

But this knowing is unconscious. To make it conscious is to become liberated. Death is seen directly, knowledge of the deathless is indirect. One who makes that direct also, comes to know that which has neither birth nor death. To attain to that life which is beyond life and death is liberation. This is present within everyone, it has only to be realized.

Someone asked a sage, "What is death and what is life? I have come to you to know this."

What the sage said in response is wonderful. He said, "Then go somewhere else. Where I am there exists neither death nor life."

54 TRANSFORMING BASER METAL INTO GOLD

YESTERDAY I SAID that dirt becomes a flower, filth and rubbish become manure and turn into fragrance. The passions and emotions of man are also like this. They are energies. What seems animalistic in man, on changing its direction, the same attains divinity.

Hence, even the mundane is divine in seed form. Then, in fact, there is nothing unholy. The whole of existence is divine. Everything is divine. The differences are only in the manifestations of that divinity.

Seen in this manner nothing remains despicable. What is animal

at one end is divine at the other. There is no contradiction between animality and divinity, but a growth. In such a context,
repression and self-torture are meaningless. That kind of struggle is
unscientific. Splitting oneself in two, no one can ever attain to
peace and self-realization.

A part of what I myself am cannot be eliminated. It may be sup-
pressed, but what is suppressed has to be continuously suppressed.
What has been overcome has to be overcome again and again.
Victory can never be achieved through that path.

The right path is entirely different. It is not of suppression, but of
knowing. It is not of discarding the filth and the rubbish – because
I am that filth and rubbish too. It is that of transforming it into
manure. This is what has been referred to in ancient alchemy as
transforming baser metal into gold.

55 Why this Fear of Death?

M AHAVIRA ASKED, "O seekers, what is the fear of living beings?"

Yesterday someone was asking me the same. And whether one asks it or not, the same question lurks in the eyes of everyone. Perhaps this is the only eternal question, and perhaps this is the only question worth asking.

Everyone is afraid. Of the known, of the unknown, fear is creeping in us. Sitting or standing, sleeping or waking, the fear continues. There is fear in all our behavior, in every thought and deed. There is fear in love, in hate, in virtue, in sin – in everything. It is as if our whole consciousness is created of fear. What else are our beliefs, concepts, religions and gods other than fear?

What is this fear? There are many forms of fear, but the fear is only one – the fear of death. That is the basic fear. At the root of all fear is the possibility of being destroyed, annihilated. Fear means the apprehension of not being, of disappearing. Effort goes on for the whole life to escape from this anxiety. All efforts are to avoid this basic insecurity.

But even after racing through one's entire life, 'being' does not become assured. The race comes to an end, but the insecurity remains the same. Life is completed, but death could not be avoided.

On the contrary, what appeared to be life turns into death on its completion. Then one comes to know it is as if there was no life at all, only death was growing. It is as if life and death were the two polarities of death itself.

Why this fear of death? Death is unknown, death is unfamiliar – how can it be feared? What connection can there be with something that is not known?

In reality, what we call the fear of death is not the fear of death, it is the fear of losing what we know as life. It is the fear of losing what is known. We have identified ourselves with what is known. That alone has become our 'is-ness', that alone has become our existence. My body, my wealth, my prestige, my relationships, my conditionings, my beliefs, my thoughts – all these have become the life of my 'I', have become my 'I'. Death will take away this 'I', that is the fear. All these are being accumulated in order to avoid fear, to gain security. But just the opposite happens – the very apprehension of losing these becomes the fear.

On the whole, whatever man does turns against the very goal for which it has been done. All steps taken in ignorance for attaining bliss take one to misery. The path taken for reaching fearlessness leads one to fear. What appears to be the attainment of the self is not the self. If one is able to wake up to this truth – if I can know that I am not what I have understood as 'I', and even in this moment I am different and separate from my identifications –

the fear disappears. Only that which is 'other' is lost in death.

In order to know this truth, no ritual, no technique is to be followed. One has only to know, only to become awake to everything one understands to be 'I', and with which one has become identified. Waking up breaks the identification. Waking up separates the self from the other. The identification of the self with the other is fear, and the realization of their separateness is freedom from fear, is fearlessness.

56 BE EMPTY OF YOURSELF

A SAGE SENT OUT THE RESIDENTS of his hermitage to travel in order to learn from the vast school of the world. When the set time was over, all of them except one returned. The sage was delighted on seeing their achievements and accumulation of knowledge. They had come back with much learning.

Eventually the other young student also returned. The sage said to him, "You have returned last of all; certainly you must have learned more than all the rest."

The young man replied, "I have returned without learning anything.

On the contrary, I have forgotten even that which you taught me." What could have been a more disappointing answer?

Then one day the same young man was massaging the body of the sage. Rubbing his back, he murmured to himself, "The temple is very beautiful, but inside it there is no image of the divine."

The sage heard it; he was outraged. Certainly these words were said to him. Certainly it is his beautiful body that has been described as a temple. Seeing the anger of the sage the young man started laughing: this was like adding fuel to the burning fire. The sage turned him out of the hermitage.

And then one morning, when the sage was reading his scriptures, the young man casually stepped in from somewhere and sat near him. He sat there as the sage continued to read. At this very moment a wild honeybee flew in the room and started searching for an exit. The door was open – the very door through which it had entered, but becoming utterly blind it was making futile efforts to go through the closed window. Its humming sound began to echo in the stillness of the temple.

Standing up, the young man said aloud to the bee, "O foolish one, there is no door there, it is a wall! Stop and look behind you – there only is the door by which you have entered."

It was not the bee, but the sage who heard these words – and he found the door. He looked into the eyes of the young man for the first time. This was not the youth who had left to go traveling.

These eyes were different. Now the sage knew that what the young man had learned was no ordinary learning. He had returned after knowing something, not after learning something.

The sage said to him, "Today I have come to know that my temple is empty of the divine, and that until now I have only been hitting my head against the wall, and I haven't found the door. Now what shall I do to find the door? What shall I do so that my temple does not remain empty of the divine?"

The young man said, "If you wish for the divine, be empty of yourself. Only he who is full of himself is empty of the divine. He who becomes empty of himself finds that he has been full with the divine forever. And if you wish to find the door to this truth, do the same that this honeybee is doing now."

The master saw that the bee was doing nothing now; it was sitting on the wall, just sitting. He understood. He woke up. He realized as though a sudden flash of lightning happened in the darkness. He also saw that the bee was now going out through the door.

This story is my whole message. This is what I am saying. Nothing has to be done to attain the divine; rather, dropping all doing, one has just to see. When the mind becomes quiet and looks, the door is found. The peaceful and empty mind is the door.

My invitation to you all is towards that emptiness. That invitation is of religion itself. To accept that invitation is to become religious.

THE WARMTH OF THE SUN has begun to spread beneath the blue sky. The cold air is thick and the dewdrops on the grass are icy cold. Dewdrops are also dripping from the flowers. *Ratrani*, the nightqueen, has gone to sleep after diffusing its fragrance the whole night long.

A cock crows and is answered by the crows in the distance. The trees are shaking gently in the mild breeze and the songs of the birds seem endless. The morning makes its mark on everything. The whole world suddenly proclaims that the day has dawned.

Seated, I watch the path that disappears among the distant trees. Slowly, slowly, the path is becoming busy and people pass by. They are walking, but they seem to be sleepy. Some inner slumber is gripping them all. They do not seem to be awake to these blissful moments of the morning, as if they have no idea that that which is behind the universe effortlessly manifests itself during these moments.

How much melody there is in life – and how deaf is man!

How much beauty there is in life – and how blind is man!

How much bliss there is in life – and how insensitive is man!

One day I had been to the hills. We stayed there for a long time, but those who had come with me were deeply engrossed in the small talk of day-to-day life – talk which has no significance, whose presence or absence in life matters not. The clouds of this talk had deprived them of the beauty of that mountain twilight.

Thus shrouded in the insignificant we remain unacquainted with the infinite, and what is in fact so close becomes far off by our own doing.

I wish to say to mankind: You have nothing to lose except your own blindness, and you have everything to gain. O, self-made beggar, open your eyes! The entire kingdom of heaven and earth is yours.

58   WAVES ARE ONLY ON THE SURFACE

YESTERDAY NOON WE WERE in a valley beneath a small mountain. Among the expanses of light and shade we spent many pleasant hours. There was a pond nearby, and powerful gusts of wind kept it restless. Waves rose, fell and dispersed. Everything in it was agitated.

Then the wind subsided and the pond was lulled to sleep.

I said, "See, one who is restless can also become peaceful. Restlessness has peace hidden within itself. The pond is peaceful now, then also it was peaceful. The waves were only on the surface; earlier, inside there was peace also."

Man too is restless only on the surface. The waves are only on the surface; inside, in the depths, a deep silence. As we move away from the winds of thoughts, the peaceful pond begins to be seen. This pond can be found now and here. There is no question of time at all, because time exists only as far as thoughts are there. Meditation is beyond time.

Jesus has said, "And there shall be time no longer."

In time is misery. Time *is* misery. To be beyond time is to be in bliss. To be beyond time is to be bliss.

Come, friend, let us go beyond time – for that is where we really are. What appears to be within time is really beyond it. Knowing this much is the going. The moment one knows, the winds stop and the pond becomes peaceful.

59 THOUGHT TOO IS 'OTHER'

I SEE MAN SURROUNDED by words, but scriptures and words are futile. That way one can know *about* the truth, but it is not the way to know truth.

Is-ness is not realized through words.

The door to is-ness is emptiness.

The very courage to take the jump from words to wordlessness is religiousness.

Thought is the means to know the other; it does not reveal the self, because the self is even behind it. Self is above everything. It is through the self that we are connected to is-ness. Thought too is other. When even that is not, then only 'that which is' manifests. Before it I am ego, in it I am Brahman.

In truth, in is-ness, self and other are eradicated. That distinction too was only in thought and of thought.

Consciousness has three aspects: 1. outer unconscious – inner unconscious; 2. outer conscious – inner unconscious, and 3. outer conscious – inner conscious.

The first aspect, unconscious, is that of non-consciousness. It is insentience. It is the pre-thought stage. The second aspect, half-unconscious, is that of half-consciousness. It is between the insentient and the sentient. This is the thought stage. The third aspect, non-unconsciousness, is that of perfect consciousness. This stage is perfectly conscious and is beyond thought.

In order to know the truth one has to attain not just to thought-lessness: that leads only to insentience, to unconsciousness. Many of the techniques prevalent in the name of religion take one only to unconsciousness. Wine, sex and music too, lead only to unconsciousness. In unconsciousness is escapism. It is not an attainment.

To attain to the truth one has to attain to both thoughtlessness *and* consciousness. This state is called *samadhi*, enlightenment.

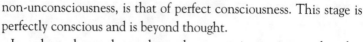

60 MAN HAS TO GIVE BIRTH TO HIMSELF

IT IS FULL-MOON NIGHT, but the sky is overcast with clouds. I have just come along a pathway. Some children were playing on a sand dune there. They had built a few sand-castles and a dispute arose among them. All disputes arise only over sand-castles. They were, after all, children, but shortly even those who were not children joined in. The elders had also joined the quarrel of the children.

I stood by the roadside and thought how superficial the division is between children and the elders! Age does not in fact bring about any difference, and maturity has no connection whatsoever with it. Most of us die as children.

There is a story about Lao Tzu, that he was born an old man. This seems very unnatural. But is not this phenomenon even more unnatural – that one may not attain to maturity till the very end of one's life? The body grows but the mind remains stagnant at one spot. That is how it is possible that there should be quarrels over sand-castles, and man reveals himself, putting aside the pretense of humanity, and proving thus that all talk of evolution is meaningless.

And who says that man has descended from animals? – he still is nothing but an animal! Is man born yet? The answer that comes after looking deeply into man is not in the affirmative.

Diogenes used to carry a burning lantern even in the broad day-light and would say, "I am searching for man."

When he became very old, someone asked him if he still hoped to find man. He said, "Yes – because I still have the burning lantern with me."

I was standing there and a big crowd gathered near the sand dune, and people were deeply enjoying and were fascinated with the insults, threats and browbeatings of the participants. There seems to be a peculiar shine in the eyes of even those who are fighting. Some animalistic pleasure is certainly flowing in their eyes and actions.

Gibran has written, "One day I asked a scarecrow standing in the middle of the field: 'Do you not get bored standing still in this field?' It replied, 'Oh, the pleasure of scaring the birds is so much that I am not at all aware how and when the time passes!' After a moment of contemplation I said: 'This is true, because I also have the experience of this pleasure.' The scarecrow said, 'Yes, only those whose body is stuffed with straw and grass can be familiar with this pleasure!"

But everybody seems to be familiar with this pleasure. Is not straw and grass stuffed inside all of us too? Are we not also false men standing in the field?

This is the pleasure I have just seen while coming back from my morning walk – the children with their sand-castles and scarecrow behavior. Is not the same pleasure going on all over the whole earth?

I ask myself this, and weep. I weep for that man who can be born but has not been born; who is within everyone but is hidden as the embers are hidden in the ashes.

In reality the body is no more than a heap of straw and grass, and for anyone who stops at that, it would have been better if he were in some field, because then at least he would have served the purpose of saving the crop from the birds. Man is not even that useful!

No one becomes really man without knowing that which is beyond the body; no one becomes man without knowing the soul. To be born in the form of man is one thing and to *be* man is entirely different.

Man has to give birth to himself within himself. It is not like garments with which one can cover oneself. No one becomes man just by covering himself with the garments of manliness, because they keep him man only so long as the actual necessity for being man does not arise. As the necessity arises, one does not even know when the garment falls off!

Just as a seed becomes a sprout by transforming its being – not by wearing any garments – similarly man also has to transmute his entire life source into a totally new dimension. Only then is he born; only then the transformation.

Then his pleasure lies not in scattering or sowing thorns, but is transformed into picking the thorns and scattering flowers. It is at this moment that it becomes evident that he is no longer straw and grass now, he is man; he is not the body, he is the soul.

Gurdjieff has said, "Drop this illusion that everyone has a soul." How does it matter whether he who is actually asleep has a soul or not? Only that is real which actually is. The soul is a possibility for all, but he alone attains it who makes it an actuality.

I FIND THE ENTIRE CONSCIOUSNESS of man revolving around three small words. What are these three words? They are: wakeful intelligence, intellect and instinct.

The most excellent beings move according to their wakeful intelligence. The mediocre move according to their intellect. The lowest state of consciousness is instinct. Instinct is animal, intellect is human, wakeful intelligence is divine.

Instinct is natural and blind. It is slumber. It is the world of the unconscious. Nothing is good or bad, there is no discrimination; hence, there is no inner struggle either. It is the natural flow of blind passions.

Intellect is neither slumber nor wakefulness. It is semi-consciousness. It is the transitory stage between instinct and wakeful intelligence. It is a corridor. A part of it has become conscious, but the rest is unconscious. Hence, there is the awareness of difference – the birth of good and bad. There is passion as well as thought.

Wakeful intelligence is total wakefulness. It is pure consciousness. It is only light. Here also is no struggle. This is natural. It is the natural flow of the good, of the true, of the beautiful.

Instinct is natural; wakeful intelligence also is natural. Instinct is blind naturalness, wakeful intelligence is awake naturalness. Only the intellect is unnatural. In intellect, towards the back is instinct and towards the front is wakeful intelligence: the crest of its flame is towards wakeful intelligence, and the roots of its base are in instinct. The surface is one thing, the depth is another. This is the tension. The temptation to drown into the animal, the challenge to rise to the divine, co-exist in intellect.

Afraid of this challenge, those who try to drown in the animal are under a delusion. The part that has become conscious cannot revert to the unconscious. In the scheme of the universe there is no path of reversion.

Accepting the challenge, those who begin to choose on the surface between good and bad are also under a delusion. That sort of choosing and change of conduct cannot be natural. It is merely an effort in acting – and that which is an effort is not good either.

The problem lies in the depths, not on the surface. That which is asleep there has to be awakened; not that the bad has to be dropped, but unconsciousness. The lamp has to be lit in the darkness.

This is my message for today.

THE STILLNESS OF NOON…the bright sunlight and drowsy trees…. I have come to sit on the grass in the shade of a roseapple tree. Now and then leaves fall on me: they seem to be the last, old leaves.

New leaves have come on all the trees. And along with the new leaves, countless numbers of new birds have also arrived. There seems to be no end to their songs. How many varieties of melodious sounds are giving music to this noon! I listen, I go on listening, and then I too slip into a unique world of music.

The world of the self is also the world of music.

This music is present in everyone; it does not have to be produced. In order to let it be audible one has only to become silent.

The moment one is silent, a veil seems to be lifted. What was always there is heard, and for the first time we realize that we are not poor. We regain the inheritance of an infinite wealth. How much does one laugh then! – the one we sought was already seated within.

63 WHAT IS, IS IMMORTAL

IT RAINED DURING THE NIGHT. The dampness still lingers and a fragrance emanates from the earth. The sun has come up high and a herd of cows is moving out to the forest. The wooden bells round their necks sound sweetly. For a while I have been listening to them. Now the cows have gone very far away and only a faint echo of the tinkling bells remains.

In the meantime, a few people have come to see me. They are asking, "What is death?"

I say, "We do not know life, hence there is death. Self-forgetfulness is death; otherwise there is no death, only a change."

Not knowing the self we have created an illusory self, and that is our 'I', the ego. It is not there, it only appears to be there. It is only this false entity that shatters. Its shattering creates misery because we are identified with it.

To realize this falsehood while living is to be saved from death. Know life, and death comes to an end. What *is*, is immortal. To know it is to attain the eternal, permanent life.

Yesterday I said the same in a meeting:

Self-knowledge is life.

Self-forgetfulness is death.

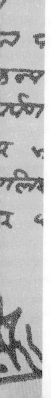

THERE IS A SCHOOLMASTER who is very much interested in religion. He has spent his life in the study of religious scriptures. If one mentions the topic of religion, there is no end to the flow of his thoughts. Like an endless string, his thoughts go on uncoiling. It is difficult to say how much he can quote and how many aphorisms he has learned by heart. No one remains unimpressed by him. He is a walking encyclopaedia, or is reputed to be so.

Many times I have heard his thoughts and have remained silent.

Once he asked me my opinion about him. I said only the truth. I said in accumulating thoughts about God, he had lost God. Certainly, he appeared to be shocked.

Later he came again to question me further in this connection. Coming to me he said, "It is only by study and contemplation that truth can be attained. There is no other way. Knowledge of course is everything."

How many people have this false notion?

I ask only one question to all such people; I asked the same to him: What is study, and what thereby happens within you? Does a dimension of new vision take birth in you? Does consciousness rise to new heights and levels? Does any revolution take place in your being? Do you become different from what you are now? Or do you remain the same with only a few more thoughts and bits of information becoming part of your memory?

Through study only the memory is trained, and on the surface of the mind more dust of thought settles. Nothing more happens, nor can happen, through it. No change happens at the center through it: the consciousness remains the same, the dimensions of experience remain the same.

To know something about truth and to know truth are two totally different things. 'To know about truth' pertains to intellect; 'to know truth' pertains to consciousness.

In order to know truth, a total awakening of consciousness – the absence of the unconscious – is essential. By training memory and so-called knowledge, this cannot happen.

What has not been known from oneself is not knowledge. The intellectual information about truth, the unknown truth, is only an appearance of knowledge. It is false and is an obstacle on the path of right-knowledge.

There is no path through the known for knowing what is in fact unknowable. It is totally new; it is such that it has never been known before. Hence, memory is not capable of delivering it, or even of recognizing it. Memory can deliver or recognize only that which has been known before. It is only a repetition of the known.

But for the arrival of the new, the entirely new, the unknown and unfamiliar, the memory has to stand aside. The memory and all known thoughts will have to stand aside so that the new may be born, so that 'what is' may be known exactly as it is. All of man's conceptions and prejudices have to stand aside for its arrival. Only the mind devoid of thoughts, memories and conceptions is conscious, is awakened. Only with an empty mind does the transformation at the center take place, and the door to truth opens up. Before this everything is a mere wandering and a waste of life.

65 ALL ATTAINING HAS TO BE DROPPED

A MONK WAS SAYING yesterday, "I have dropped all worldly desires. Now my interest is only in liberation, and this alone is freedom. Interest in the world is withdrawal from liberation; interest in liberation is withdrawal from the world."

How true and full of wisdom the statement seems to be; there seems to be no flaw in it anywhere. It appeals totally to the intellect and logic, but it is actually meaningless. In such word games, so many people remain deceived. As far as spiritual life is concerned, intellect and logic do not seem to take one anywhere.

I said to him, "You are entangled in words. 'Worldly desires' does not mean anything. Actually, desire itself *is* worldly, for what makes no difference. The very existence of desire is worldly: whether or not it is towards the world or liberation, its nature is the same."

Desire takes man away from himself. It is passion, it is greed for some gain, it is a yearning and a race to become something. **A** desires to become **B**, this is its nature. And as long as there is a desire to become something, that which is is not revealed. The revelation of is-ness is liberation.

Liberation is not a thing which has to be achieved; it is not an object of desire. Hence, there can be no longing towards it. It happens when all longings cease, even those for liberation. Then that which is, is called liberation. So liberation is not to be attained. In fact, all attaining has to be dropped and then...*then* liberation is attained.

66 ONLY THE SEEING REMAINS

WHAT MAN CALLS 'THE UNIVERSE' is not the limit of existence, it is only the limit of man's senses. Beyond these senses is a limitless expanse. This limitless expanse can never be attained through the senses, because the senses perceive only a fragment, only a part. And what is limitless, infinite, cannot be subjected to fragmentation and division. No limited means can measure that which is limitless. What is limitless can be grasped only through the limitless.

And those who have known it have not known it through their senses or their intellect: they have known it by becoming limitless themselves.

This is possible, because in the seemingly insignificant and limited man, the limitless too is present. Man does not end at the senses, nor is he only his senses. He is spread in dimensions beyond the senses. What is seen is the point of his beginning, but not the limit of his end. He is invisible: the invisible is seated within the circumference of the visible.

If a man realizes the invisible within himself, he realizes the entire universe. All divisions and fragments are related to the visible. The invisible is unfragmented – the one and the many are the same. And this is why in attaining the one, the all is attained.

Mahavira has said, "One who has known one has known all." That one is within. That one is the seer, not the seen. Hence, the eyes are not the means for realizing it, closing the eyes is the way.

Closing the eyes means freedom from the visible. If the visible flows even before the closed eye, know that the eye is as good as open. If the visible is not in sight, the eye may be open, but it is as good as closed. When there is no seen and only the seeing remains, the seer appears.

The seeing in which one sees the seer is right-seeing. Without right-seeing, man is blind. Having eyes, he has no sight. Sight is attained through right-seeing – the real eye, the eye that is beyond the senses. Then boundaries disappear, the lines of division are no more, and that which is – the beginningless and the endless expanse, Brahman – is attained.

This attainment is liberation, because every limitation is a bondage, every limitation is dependence. To go beyond limitation is to become free.

67 KNOWING BEGINS WITH LOVING ONESELF

I HEARD A DISCOURSE YESTERDAY: its essence was 'self-suppression'. This is the popular tradition. It is thought that one has to love everybody but hate oneself; one has to create enmity with oneself, then possibly self-conquest can happen. But this thought is as incorrect as it is popular. On this path, one's personality splits into two, and violence with oneself begins – and violence makes everything ugly.

Man does not have to suppress his passions in this way, nor is it possible. The path of violence is not the path of religion. It is due to this that so many ways of torturing the body have developed. The torture appears to be penance, but in reality it is the sadistic pleasure of violence, suppression and resistance.

This is not penance, this is self-deception.

Man has not to fight with himself, he has to know himself.

But the knowing begins with loving oneself.

One has to love oneself in a right manner. The man who blindly follows his passions does not love himself, nor does the man who blindly fights with them. They both are blind; the second blindness is born in reaction to the first one. One man ruins himself in his passions, the other in fighting with them. They are both full of hatred towards themselves.

Knowledge begins with loving oneself: "Whatever I am is to be accepted, is to be loved". It is only in this acceptance and love that the light is attained through which all is transformed naturally, and a fresh beauty arises in the individual – a music, a peace, a bliss. The integrated effect of all these is called spiritual life.

68 I HAVE NO OPINION

SOME DISCUSSION ABOUT TRUTH is going on when I arrive. I listen to it. The people who are talking are studious. They are conversant with schools of philosophy: how many thought systems there are, how many viewpoints – it all seems to be known to them. Their minds are full, not with the truth, but with what others have said about the truth – as if truth can be known on the basis of what others have said; as if truth is a viewpoint, a thought, or some intellectual, logical conclusion! Their debate is deepening and now no one is in a state to listen to anybody. Everyone is speaking, but no one is listening.

I am silent. Then someone remembers me, and they all want to know my opinion too. I have no opinion. I see that where there is opinion there is no truth. Truth begins where thought ends.

What shall I say? They are eager to hear. I tell them a story:

There was a mystic, Bodhidharma. In the sixth century A.D., he went to China. He stayed there for some years. Then he wished to return home and he gathered all his disciples. He wanted to know how far they had progressed in the realm of truth.

In reply to his query a disciple said, "In my opinion, truth is beyond acceptance and non-acceptance. Neither can it be said that it is, nor can it be said that it is not – because such is its nature."

Bodhidharma said, "It is my skin that you have."

The second disciple said, "As I see it, truth is an insight. Once attained it is attained forever. It cannot be lost."

Bodhidharma said, "It is my flesh that you have."

The third disciple said, "I consider that the five basic elements are as nothing and the five *skandhas* – forms of mundane consciousness – are unreal. This very nothingness is truth."

Bodhidharma said, "It is my bones that you have."

Then arose one who knew; he put his head at the feet of his master and remained silent. He was quiet and his eyes were empty.

Bodhidharma said, "It is my marrow, my soul, that you have."

And this story itself is my answer.

69 THERE IS NO ANSWER OUTSIDE

I WENT TO A TEMPLE to give a talk. After my talk, a young man said, "Can I ask a question? I have asked this question to many, but the answers I received do not satisfy me. All systems of philosophy say, 'Know thyself.' I too want to know myself. And this alone is my question: 'Who am I?' I desire an answer for this very question."

I said, "You haven't yet asked the question, how could you have received an answer? Asking the question is not so easy."

For a moment the young man looked at me in amazement. It was clear that he had not understood the implications of my statement. He said, "What is this you say, that I haven't asked the question yet?"

I told him, "Come to me at night." He came to me that night. He might have thought I would give him some answer. I did give him an answer, but the answer I gave he would never have thought of.

He came. As soon as he sat, I put off the light. He said, "What are you doing? Do you give answers in darkness?"

I said, "I do not give an answer, I only teach you how to ask the question. Regarding spiritual life and truth, there is no answer outside. Knowledge is not an external fact, it is not a piece of information – hence it cannot be put into you from outside. It has to be drawn out from within, even as water is drawn out from a well. It is eternal, it is ever-present; we have only to open our vessel to it. The only thing to be remembered in this process is that the vessel is empty. If the vessel is empty it comes back filled up, and one has attained."

In the darkness, a little time passed in silence. Then he said, "Now what shall I do?"

I said, "Empty the vessel, be quiet and ask: 'Who am I?' Ask once, twice, thrice, ask with total force: 'Who am I?' Let the question ring and echo through your entire being and then remain quiet and silent, waiting thoughtlessly. Question and then silence, an empty awaiting. This is the procedure.

He said after a short while, "But I am not able to remain quiet. I have asked the question, but a silent waiting is impossible, and now I am able to see that I had never actually asked the question until today."

70 TO THE VERY PIT OF THE UNCONSCIOUS

I AM READING A DISCOURSE from some saint. He has urged people to abandon anger, to abandon attachment, to abandon passions – as if these were things which could be abandoned! As if one wished to shake them off and could just abandon them! However, reading and hearing create this impression.

Looking at such sermons one comes to realize, how dense is our ignorance and how little we know about the human mind!

I said to a child one day, "Why don't you drop your illness?" The boy began to laugh and said, "Is it within my power to drop the illness?"

Every person wants to drop illness and evil – but it is necessary to dive deep to the roots of the evil, it is necessary to go to the very pit of the unconscious from where they emerge. One cannot become free of them merely by making a resolution in the conscious mind.

Freud has narrated an interesting event. A villager was staying at a city hotel. In the night he tried to put out the light in his room, but he did not succeed. He tried to blow out the light again and again, but the light shone without even a flicker. Next morning he made a complaint about it. In answer to the complaint, he came to find out that the light was not a conventional lamp that could be blown out, it was an electric light.

And I say that it is a wrong procedure to ask people to blow out their evil emotions and feelings. They are not earthen lamps, they are electric lamps. The process of extinguishing them lies hidden in the unconscious.

All resolutions of the conscious mind are futile, like an attempt to blow out the electric lamp. Only by descending into the unconscious through some suitable medium can their roots be cut.

TICK...TICK...TICK...the clock has started running again. In fact, it has been running all along – only for me it had stopped. Or, better to say, I myself had become closed to the space where this running exists.

I had moved into another realm of time. I was sitting with eyes closed, looking within, and went on looking – it was altogether a different realm of time. Then contact with this realm was broken.

How blissful it is to slip out of time! Pictures in the mind stop. Their existence is time. As they cease, time ceases and then only the pure present remains. The present is part of time only in language. In reality, it is outside the realm of time, beyond it. To be in it is to be in the self. I have returned from that world now. How peaceful everything is! In the distance some bird is singing, a child is crying in the neighborhood and a cock is crowing.

How blissful it is to live! And now I know that death too is blissful, because life does not end with it. It is only a state of life – life is before it and after it also.

72 CONSCIOUSNESS IS GOD

W HAT IS GOD?

In how many minds does this question arise! Yesterday a young man was asking me – and this question is asked as if God is a thing, separate and different from the seeker, and as if it can be obtained like other things. The very idea of attaining God is futile, and also the idea of understanding him – because he is in one's every cell. One is in him. To say it more correctly: I am not, only he is.

God is the name of that which is. He is not something within is-ness, he himself *is* that which is. He does not possess existence, rather the very existence is in him. He is the name of that which is, of existence, of the nameless.

Hence he is not sought, because the seeker himself is in him.

One can only get lost in him.

And to get lost is to attain him.

There is a tale: A fish was fed up with hearing the name of the ocean again and again. One day she asked the queen of fishes, "I have been hearing the name of the ocean for so long, but what is this ocean? And where is it?"

The queen said, "In the ocean is your birth, your life, your very world. The ocean is your very is-ness. The ocean is within you and without you. You are made of ocean and in ocean is your end. The ocean surrounds you every moment."

God surrounds everyone each moment, but we are unconscious – hence he is not seen.

Unconsciousness is the world, consciousness is God.

73 ONE HAS ONLY TO KNOW UNREST

AN ASCETIC CAME, he has been a sannyasin for years. I asked him, "Why did you take sannyas?" He said, "I desired peace."

This made me think: can even peace be desired? Are not peace and desire contradictory to each other? I said so to him.

He looked a little puzzled. He said, "What shall I do then?"

I began to laugh. I said, "Is not desire hidden in doing, too?"

The question is not of doing something. Nothing can be done for peace. It is not a part of desire, it is futile to desire it. In fact, it is necessary to understand unrest. What is unrest? This has to be known – not through scriptures, but for oneself. It is because of reading the scriptures that the desire for peace arises, and so the question 'what should be done?' arises.

The ascetic said, "Unrest is due to passions, due to desires. If the desire ceases, there is peace."

I said, "This answer is from the scriptures, not your own; otherwise it would not have been possible to say, 'I desire peace.' If desire is unrest, how then can peace be desired? Just know the unrest, wake up to it through self-experience, understand it through an innocent, unbiased mind. This understanding will bring the roots of unrest in front of you. Passion is the root of unrest – this will be seen by you. And this very seeing becomes the disappearance of unrest.

Becoming aware of the unrest is its death. Its life is possible only in darkness and in blindness. The moment the light of knowing enters, it ceases to exist. What remains with the disappearance of unrest is peace.

Peace is not to be desired against unrest. Peace is not the opposite of unrest, it is the absence of unrest. Hence, one has not to seek peace, one has only to know unrest. Borrowed knowledge from scriptures becomes an obstacle to this knowing of unrest, because ready-made answers fill the mind with borrowed conclusions before one can ever experience. No transformation happens through these borrowed conclusions; self-experience is the path. In his spiritual life, every individual has to tread the path for himself – after unloading the burden of borrowed knowledge.

WHAT HAS HAPPENED to man?

I get up in the morning – I see the squirrels running about, I see the flowers opening up in the rays of the sun, I see nature overflowing with harmonious melody. I go to bed at night – I see the silence showering from the stars, I see the blissful sleep encompassing the entire creation. And then I begin to ask myself, "What has happened to man?"

Everything is vibrating with bliss except man. Everything is resonating with music except man. Everything is settled in divine peace except man. Is man not a participant in all this? Is man an outsider, a stranger? This strangeness has been fashioned by his own hands. He has created this rupture with his own hands.

I am reminded of the biblical story. After eating the 'fruit of knowledge' man is driven out from paradise. How true this story is! Knowledge, intellect, the mind have torn man apart from life. Remaining in existence, he has fallen out of it.

As soon as one drops knowledge, as soon as one drops mind, then a new world unfolds. In it, we become one with nature. Nothing is separate there, nothing is different. Everything begins to throb in a melodious music of peace.

This experience alone is 'God'.

God is not a person, God is not experienced. Rather, the experience itself is called God. God is not seen face to face, rather the direct seeing itself is called God.

In this direct seeing, man becomes healthy and whole. In this experience he comes home. In this light he becomes a participant in the natural bliss of the plants and the flowers. In all this, he disappears at one end and attains to is-ness at the other. This is his death as well as his rebirth.

75 WHEN SEEKING AND THE SEEKER CEASE

SOMEONE WAS ASKING, "How to attain to atman, the soul? How to attain to Brahman, the ultimate reality?"

As far as I can see, the very idea of attaining the soul is wrong. It is not something yet to be attained, it is already eternally attained. It is not a thing that has to be brought in, it is not an aim which has to be realized, it is not in the future that one has to reach up to it – it *is*. Its name is 'that which is'. It is present, eternally present. There is no past or future in it. There is no becoming in it, neither is it possible to lose it; nor has the idea of attaining it any meaning. It is the pure, eternal existence.

Then on what level has this losing taken place? Or, from where has come this appearance of losing and the thirst for attaining?

If one understands the 'I', then the losing of the soul – which really cannot be lost – can be understood. 'I' is not the soul. Neither is the 'self' nor the 'other' the soul. This duality is of thought, this duality is of the mind.

Mind is an apparent entity. It is never in the present. It is either in the past or in the future, and neither of the two have any existence: the one has already become non-existent, the other has not yet come into existence. The one is in our memory, the other in our imagination, but both are non-existent. Out of this non-existence the 'I' is born.

The 'I' is the product of thought. Time too is the product of thought. Because of thought, because of the 'I', the soul is covered. It is, but it appears to have been lost. Then this very 'I', this very thought-stream, sets out to search for this so-called lost soul. This search is impossible, because through this search the 'I' becomes more and more nourished and strengthened.

Searching for the soul through the 'I' is like searching for awakening through dreams. One has to attain it not through the 'I', but through the disappearance of the 'I'. When the dream disappears, awakening *is*. When the 'I' disappears, soul *is*.

The soul is nothingness because it is wholeness. There is no 'self' or 'other' in it. It is non-dual, it is beyond time. The moment thought ceases and the mind disappears, it is discovered that the soul has never been lost.

Hence, it is not to be sought.

The seeking is to be dropped, and the one who seeks is to be dropped. When seeking and the seeker cease, the search is complete. It is attained by losing the 'I'.

76 THIS IS REAL HOLINESS

WHAT IS HOLINESS?

The question arises in the minds of many. If holiness had anything to do with a certain kind of clothing and external appearance, the very question would not have arisen. Certainly holiness is not an external reality, it is some internal reality. What is this internal reality?

Holiness is being in oneself. Ordinarily man is outside himself, not even for a moment is he in himself. He is with everyone, but not with himself. This very separation from the self is the unholiness. Coming back to the self, being rooted in one's own self, becoming healthy, is holiness. Spiritual unhealth is unholiness, spiritual health is holiness.

If I am outside myself, I am asleep. The external is the 'other', is unconsciousness. Mahavira has said, "He who is asleep is the non-sage." To wake up from the dependence of the 'other' into the freedom of the 'self' is to be holy.

How is this holiness recognized?

This holiness is recognized by the peace, by the bliss, by the wholeness.

There was a saint – Saint Francis. He was on a pilgrimage with his disciple Leo. They were on their way to San Marino when they were caught up in a rainstorm. They got completely soaked and covered with mud. Night was setting in, and the day-long hunger and travel-weariness had overwhelmed them. The village was still far off and it was not possible to reach there before midnight. Suddenly Saint Francis said, "Leo, who is the real saint? Not he who can give eyes to the blind, who can give health to the sick and can even raise up the dead – he is not the real saint."

There was silence for a while. Then Francis spoke again: "Leo, the real saint is not the one who can understand the language of the animals, trees, stones and rocks. Not even he who has acquired the knowledge of the whole world is a real saint."

There was silence again for a while. They kept on moving in the middle of the rainstorm. Now the lights of San Marino were visible. Saint Francis spoke again: "...Nor is the one who has renounced all a real saint."

Now Leo could not remain silent anymore. He asked, "Then who is the true saint?"

Saint Francis replied, "We are about to reach San Marino and will knock at the outer door of the inn. The watchman will ask, 'Who is there?' We will reply, 'Your own two brothers, two ascetics.' If he were to say then, 'You beggars, wretched mendicants, lazy parasites – get away, get away! There is no place for you here!'; and if he refused to open the door, and hungry, tired, covered with mud we continue to stay in the middle of the night, out in the open, and we knock at the door again; if at this time he were to come out, hit us with a baton and say, 'You scoundrels, do not disturb us!'; if nothing moves within us on this occasion too; if everything within remains peaceful, calm and empty, and in that innkeeper we continue to see nothing but the divine – then this is real holiness."

Certainly, to attain to the state of undisturbed peace, simplicity and equanimity under all circumstances is holiness.

L AST NIGHT A YOUNG MAN asked, "I am fighting against my mind, but I am unable to attain peace. What shall I do with the mind so that I may attain peace?"

I said, "No one can do anything with darkness, it simply does not exist. It is only the absence of light, hence, fighting against it is ignorance."

So is the mind: that too does not exist. That too does not have any existence of its own. It is the absence of self-realization, it is the absence of meditation; hence, nothing can be done with it directly. If darkness is to be removed, one has to bring light in. Similarly, if the mind is to be removed, meditation has to be brought in.

The mind is not to be controlled – but it is to be realized that mind simply does not exist! The moment this is realized, one is free of it.

He asked, "How to realize this?"

"This realization happens through a witnessing consciousness. Be a witness of the mind. Be a witness of what is, drop the worry of how it should be. What is, as it is – awaken to it, be alert to it. Do not judge, do not control, do not fall in any struggle – just watch silently. This watching, this witness itself becomes the liberation."

The moment one becomes a witness, consciousness leaves the seen and settles on the seer. In this state is attained the unwavering flame of wisdom. And this very flame is liberation.

78 REMOVING DUST FROM A MIRROR

I HAVE FOUND AN OLD MIRROR lying in a corner. Dust has completely covered it. It does not appear to still be a mirror which would be able to catch reflections, because the dust has covered everything and the mirror has become almost hidden. It appears that only the dust is and the mirror is not. But in getting covered by the dust, is the mirror really destroyed? The mirror is still a mirror, nothing has changed in it. The dust is on the mirror and not in it. The dust has become a screen, a cover; it does not destroy. A screen only covers, it does not destroy – and as soon as this screen is removed, that which is becomes manifest again.

I said to someone that man's consciousness is also like this mirror: the dust of passions is spread over it. There is a screen of emotions over it, there are layers of thoughts over it, but nothing has changed in the nature of the consciousness. It is the same. It is always the same. Whether there is a screen or not, there is no change in it. All screens are only on the surface, hence pulling them aside and removing them is not a difficult thing. Removing dust from consciousness is not any more difficult than removing dust from a mirror.

It is easy to attain to the soul, because there is no other obstacle in between except a thin screen of dust. And as the screen is removed, it is immediately realized that the soul itself is God.

79 PHOTOS PROJECTED ON THE SCREEN

I HAVE RETURNED FROM A MOVIE showing. It is surprising to see how much the light and shade photos projected on the screen captivate people. Where there is really nothing, everything happens! I watched the audience there, and it felt as if they had forgotten themselves, as if they were not there, but the flow of electrically projected pictures was everything.

A blank screen is in front and from the back the pictures are being projected. Those who are watching it have their eyes fixed in front, and no one is aware of what is happening behind their backs.

This is how the *leela*, the play, is born.

This is what happens both within man and without.

There is a projector at the back of the human mind. Psychology calls this back-side the unconscious. The longings, the passions, the conditionings accumulated in this unconscious are being continuously projected onto the mind's screen. This flow of mental projections goes on every moment, non-stop.

The consciousness is a seer, a witness, and it forgets itself in this flow of the pictures, of desires. This forgetfulness is ignorance. This ignorance is the root cause of *maya*, illusion, and the endless cycle of birth and death. Waking up from this ignorance happens in the cessation of the mind. When the mind is devoid of thoughts, when the flow of pictures on the screen stops, only then the onlooker remembers himself and returns to his home.

Patanjali calls this cessation of the activities of the mind Yoga. If this is achieved, all is achieved.

80 HAPPINESS IS NOT RELIGION

YESTERDAY I WAS STANDING at the door of a temple. Incense was burning and the whole atmosphere was fragrant. Then the bells of worship started ringing and the lamp of propitiation was being waved in front of the idol. Some devotees were there. The entire arrangement was beautiful and was producing a pleasant trance, but all these rituals have nothing to do with religion.

No temple, no mosque, no church, no form of worship, no form of prayer has anything to do with religion. All the idols are stones and all the prayers are nothing but empty words addressed to the walls.

But some happiness seems to be coming from all this – and that is the danger, because it is due to this that a great deception begins and crystalizes. It is in this illusion of happiness that the appearance of truth is born. This happiness is derived through unconsciousness – forgetfulness of oneself and escape from the reality of oneself. The happiness of intoxicants also comes from such an escape. All acts of unconsciousness in the name of religion bring only a false happiness, like that of intoxicants. Happiness is not religion, because it is only the forgetfulness of sorrow, not its end.

What, then, is religion?

Religion is not an escape *from* oneself, it is an awakening *towards* oneself. This awakening has no connection with any external arrangements. It is related to moving inwards and attaining consciousness.

To wake up and become a witness, to become conscious of that which is – religion is related only with this. Religion is non-unconsciousness, and non-unconsciousness is bliss.

81 "IS THAT SO?"

THERE IS A STORY.

An unmarried girl became pregnant. Her relatives were at their wit's end: they asked her about the person who was responsible for it. She said that the ascetic staying outside the village had raped her. The infuriated relatives surrounded the ascetic and berated him. The ascetic calmly listened to their outbursts and said simply, "Is that so?" He spoke only this much, and then volunteered to take on the responsibility of the child's upbringing.

On returning home, the girl felt a deep remorse and she confessed the truth. She said she had never even seen the ascetic, and that she had lied only to protect the real father of the child. Her relatives felt a deep remorse too. They went and apologized to the ascetic and asked for his forgiveness. The ascetic listened to the whole thing calmly and said, "Is that so?"

When peace descends in one's life, this entire world and its events remain nothing more than acting. I become a mere actor. The story goes on moving on the outside, and the inside remains shrouded in a nothingness. Only after attaining to this state can the liberation from slavery to the world happen.

I am a slave if I am agitated by whatever comes from outside – if anybody from outside can affect and alter my inside. In this way, I am dependent. If I become liberated from the outside – no matter what happens on the outside, I remain the same – it marks the beginning of self and freedom.

This liberation begins with the attainment of nothingness.

We have to become a zero.

We have to experience the emptiness.

Walking or sleeping, sitting or getting up, one has to know, "I am an emptiness," and keep remembrance of it. By keeping remembrance of the emptiness one becomes empty. The emptiness fills your every single breath. When the emptiness comes within, simplicity comes on the outside. Emptiness itself is godliness.

82 WHAT IS SEEN WITH THE EYES CLOSED

I WAS SITTING WITH MY EYES CLOSED. Always seeing with the eyes open, man is forgetting the art of seeing with closed eyes. What is seen with open eyes is nothing compared to what is seen with the eyes closed. The tiny eyelid separates and joins two worlds.

I was sitting with eyes closed when a person came: he asked me what I was doing. When I said I was seeing something, he became almost perplexed. Perhaps he would have thought, "Can seeing with closed eyes be called seeing?"

When I open my eyes I arrive in the finite. When I close my eyes, the doors of the infinite open. On one side one sees the seen and on the other, the seer.

There was a mystic woman, Rabiya. On a beautiful morning somebody had said to her, "Rabiya, what are you doing inside the hut? Come out! See here, what a beautiful morning God has created!"

Rabiya replied from inside the hut, "Here inside, I am seeing the creator of the morning that you are seeing outside. Friend, you had better come in. No external beauty has any meaning before the beauty that is here."

But how many people remain outside even after closing their eyes? The eyes are not closed just by shutting them. The eyes are closed, but the external pictures are still forming. The eyelids are shut, but the external scenes are still descending. This is not the closing of the eyes.

The closing of the eyes means emptiness, freedom from dreams and thoughts. When thoughts and scenes disappear, the eyes are closed. What then manifests is the eternal consciousness. That is truth, that is consciousness, that is bliss. The whole game is of the eyes. The eye transformed, everything is transformed.

A YEAR HAS PASSED SINCE I sowed some seeds. Now flowers have come. How much I yearned for the flowers to come directly, but they do not come out that way. If one wants flowers, one has to sow seeds, one has to look after the plants, and then in the end one sees the long awaited. This process is true not only about flowers but also about life.

Non-violence, non-possessivness, non-stealing, truth and celibacy – these are the flowers born of right-living. Nobody can bring them directly. In order to bring them we have to sow the seed of self-realization. As soon as that comes, all these follow on their own.

Self-realization is the root, all the rest is its outcome. Ugliness in the external behavior is a symbol of inner corruption, while beauty is the echo of the inner life and its music. Hence nothing can be attained by changing the symptoms. The change has to be effected where the roots of evil basically are.

Ignorance of the self is the root of evil. Who am I? – this is to be known. The moment this is known, fearlessness and non-duality are attained. The realization of non-duality – the awareness that the other is the same as I am – burns up all violence from its very roots, and as a result of this, non-violence appears.

Knowing the other as 'other' is violence. Seeing the self in the other is non-violence, and non-violence is the soul of religion.

84 ONLY BLISS CAN BE ETERNAL

IT RAINED LAST NIGHT and I came inside. The windows were all shut and there was a feeling of suffocation. Then I opened the windows and a freshness blew in with the freshly bathed gusts of the wind. When I sank into deep sleep, I know not.

In the morning a man came to visit. Seeing him, I was reminded of the suffocation of the previous night. It felt as if all the windows and all the doors of his mind were closed; he had not left even a single window open from where fresh air and light might enter. Everything in him was closed. I was talking to him and feeling as if I was talking to the walls! Then it came to me, that the majority of people are similarly closed and are deprived of the beauty, the freshness and the newness of life.

Man turns himself into a prison on his own. He feels the suffocation and frustration of the imprisonment but he is unable to figure out its root cause – the original source of boredom and anxiety. His whole life passes like this. One who could have had the ecstasy of a flight in the open sky, dies shut in a parrot-cage.

On demolishing the walls of the mind, the open sky is attained. And this open sky is life. Everybody can attain this liberation, and everybody *has* to attain this liberation.

I say this every day, but perhaps my words do not reach everybody. Their walls are strong – but howsoever strong their walls, they themselves are basically weak and full of pain. The only glimmer of hope is that they are full of pain, and what is painful cannot be sustained for long. Only bliss can be eternal.

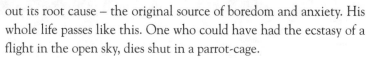

85 THERE IS REAL LIFE

THE DOMES OF THE TEMPLES are shining in the sunlight. The sky is clear and the throng of people on the road is getting thicker and thicker. I see the people walking on the road, and I don't know why they do not appear to be alive. How can one be called alive if one is not aware of life, of existence? Life begins and comes to an end, but it seems we do not notice it. Generally we become aware of life when the moment of death arrives.

I have read a story:

There was a person who was incurably forgetful – he had forgotten that he was alive! One morning he got up and realized that he was dead, then he realized that he was once alive too.

There is a great truth in this story. I am reminded of this story, and I have a hearty laugh over the fact that through death somebody had realized that he was once alive. But my laughter slowly turns into sadness over this pitiful situation.

I am thinking all this when some visitors arrive. I look at them, I listen to their words and I look into their eyes. There is no life anywhere in them. They are like shadows.

The whole world has become filled with shadows. The majority of people are living in a world of ghosts they themselves have created. And there *is* a spark, there is life in these shadows, but they are not aware of that. There is real life within this shadow-life, and there is true life beyond this ghost-life, which can be attained right now and right here.

How small is the condition for attaining this!

How easy is the means for attaining this!

As I said yesterday: the seeing is to be directed withinwards.

A YOUNG MAN CAME and said, "I have become an atheist." I look at him. I know him from before. His thirst for knowing the truth of life is acute: he wants to experience the truth at any cost. He has a sharp genius, and superficial faiths do not satisfy him. Conditionings, traditions and conventions are unable to offer him anything. He is covered in doubts and suspicions, all mental props and convictions have shattered, and he has sunk into deep negativity from all this.

I am silent. He speaks once again, "My faith in God has gone. There is no God. I have become irreligious."

I ask him, "Please, don't say so. Becoming an atheist is not becoming irreligious. One has to pass through a phase of negation to attain to real theism. It is the beginning of becoming really religious and not of becoming irreligious. Theism, inherited through conditionings, education and thoughts, is no theism at all: he who is content with it is in delusion. Had he been brought up in the midst of some opposite school of thought, his mind would have been shaped in the opposite way and he then would have been content with that alone.

"Conditionings of the mind are a phenomenon at the circumference, at the surface. It is a dead layer. It is a borrowed and stale state. A person really thirsty for spiritual life cannot quench his thirst with this imaginary water. In this sense that person is blessed, because the search for the real water begins with this unquenched thirst. Thank God that you do not agree with the concept of God, because this disagreement can lead you to the truth of God."

I now see a glow spreading across the face of that youth. A peace, an assurance has descended in his eyes. While he takes leave of me I tell him, "Remember this much, that atheism is the beginning of a religious life. It is not an end, it is a background, but one has not to halt there. It is a dark night, but one has not to be drowned in it. It is after this, through this, that the dawn appears."

87 DROP ALL DOING

LAST NIGHT, away from the city, we were sitting in a mango grove. There were some clouds in the sky and the moon played hide-and-seek among them. In this play of light and shadow, some people were silently there with me for a long time.

How difficult it becomes to speak sometimes! When the atmosphere is thick with a melody, a music, one is afraid to speak lest it should be disrupted. So it happened last night. We returned home very late. On the way, someone remarked, "This is the first time in my life that I have experienced silence. I had heard that silence is a wonderful bliss, but I realized it only today. Today it has happened effortlessly – but how will it happen again?"

I said, "What has happened effortlessly happens only effortlessly; it does not happen with effort."

Effort itself is unrest. Effort means that something different from what is, is being wished for. This state is of tension. Only tension is born out of tension. Anything done in unrest brings only unrest. Unrest does not turn into peace.

Peace is a different state of consciousness.

When unrest is not, peace is.

Do not do anything, do not make any effort; drop all doing and remain just watching. Then it is found that a new consciousness, a new light, is descending slowly, slowly.

What is found in this new world is what really is.

The revelation of that which is, is bliss, is liberation.

This cosmic immensity does not arrive through our tiny efforts, through our 'I', but rather it comes when there are no efforts, when 'I' is not.

Whatever is attained in the world is attained through doing, through actions. Effort is the means, 'I' is the center. Hence every attainment strengthens the 'I'. In fact, the happiness in attainment is that of strengthening and expanding the 'I'. But this 'I' is never wholly filled, it is insatiable by its very nature. Hence, happiness only appears to be there, in fact it is never achieved. Hence, those who know say that there is nothing but sorrow in the world.

What we do in the world, we do the same for liberation also. We get busy in achieving liberation, and that is where the error is. It is not to be attained; rather one has to lose oneself. As one loses oneself, it is attained.

88 ATTAINING THE RIGHT VISION

LAST NIGHT, I WAS on the riverbank for a long time. The river, shining like a silver ribbon, wound its way far into the distance. A fisherman had come rowing his small boat, and hearing his sounds the water birds which had long been warbling became quiet.

A friend was with me. He sang a devotional song and then the conversation moved to the topic of God. The theme of the song was also the quest for God. Many years of the singer's life had gone into the search for God. I met him only yesterday. He has a bachelor's degree in science; and then one day the quest for God seized him. Many years have gone in the quest since then, but nothing has been attained.

After listening to the devotional song, I was quiet. His voice was sweet and touched the heart; and his heart was behind the song, so the song had become alive. Its echo was reverberating in my heart. But disrupting the silence, he spontaneously asked if the quest for God was only a delusion. "I was full of hope in the beginning," he said, "but slowly, slowly, I have become disillusioned."

I still kept quiet for a while, and then said, "The quest for God *is* an illusion because the very question of search does not arise. He is ever-present, but we do not have the eyes that can see him. So the real search is for attaining the right vision."

There was a blind man: he went out in search of the sun. His quest was wrong. The sun is already there, it is the eyes that are to be sought. As one attains the eyes, the sun is attained. Usually the seeker for God engages himself in seeking God directly. He does not give even a single thought about his eyes. This basic mistake brings disappointment as the outcome.

My observation is just the opposite: I see that the real question is about me and is of my transformation. As I am, as my eyes are – that alone is the limit of my knowledge and the limit of my seeing. If I change – if my eyes change – if my consciousness changes, then what is invisible also becomes visible. And then God is attained in the depths of the very things we are seeing now; God is attained in the world itself. That is why I say: religion is not a science of attaining God but of attaining a new vision, a new consciousness. God already is, we are rooted in him alone, we are living in him alone; we do not have eyes, so the sun is not visible to us. One has not to seek for the sun, but for eyes.

89 THE FIFTH NOBLE TRUTH IS THE FIRST

GAUTAM BUDDHA HAS PROPOUNDED four noble truths: suffering, the cause of suffering, the possibility of the elimination of suffering, and the path to the elimination of suffering. There is suffering in life, there is the cause of suffering; this suffering can be eliminated, and there is a path to eliminate it.

I see a fifth noble truth also, which existed prior to the four. These four exist because the fifth one exists. But for its prior existence, the other four too could not have been there.

What is that fifth – or rather, the first – noble truth?

That truth is: our unconsciousness of our suffering. There is suffering, but we are unconscious of it. It is because of this unconsciousness that we live in suffering – but it does not distress us. The whole of our life passes by in this foggy unconsciousness, in this drowsiness, and the suffering is thus endured.

In this unconsciousness, what is does not come to our eyes and the dreams of what is not continue. There is a blindness towards the present and the eyes are focused on the future. In the intoxication of the pleasant dreams of the future, the suffering of the present lies submerged. With this method, the suffering is not seen, and the very question of going beyond it does not arise.

If a prisoner does not realize his chains and the walls of the jail, where is the source of yearning for freedom in him? Hence, I call this truth the first noble truth – the truth that we are unconscious of suffering.

The truth that life is suffering is not in our consciousness: the other four follow this. They are seen as I wake up to suffering.

90 THE DIAGNOSIS IS ITSELF THE REMEDY

I SAY ONLY A FEW THINGS; they can be counted on the fingers.

One: the mind has to be known – the mind that is so close and yet so unknown.

Two: the mind has to be transformed – the mind that is so stubborn and yet so eager to be transformed!

Three: the mind has to be liberated – the mind that is wholly in bondage but which can be liberated here and now.

These things are three only in name. Really, only one thing is to be done, and that is to know the mind. The other two are accomplished on their own when this first is accomplished. Knowing is the only transformation, knowing is the only liberation.

I was saying this yesterday, when someone asked, "How is this knowing to happen?"

This knowing happens through waking up. Our activities of both body and mind are unconscious. It is necessary to wake up to each activity – whether one is walking or sitting or lying down, one should have right-remembrance of it. "I wish to sit" – one has to wake up to this wish, to this feeling as well. Whether there is anger in the mind or not, one has to watch this state too. If thoughts are moving or not, one has to become a witness to that also.

This waking up cannot be attained through suppression or struggle: there has to be no judgment, no choosing between good and bad. Only waking up, just waking up! As soon as one wakes up, the mystery of the mind is revealed – the mind is known. And just by knowing, the transformation comes. By complete knowing the liberation happens.

Hence, I say that liberation from the disease of the mind is easy, because the diagnosis is itself the remedy.

91 SEEING, NOT LEARNING, IS KNOWLEDGE

THE AFTERNOON IS ALMOST GONE. The sky was clear, but strong winds came and it is getting covered with thick, black clouds. The sun is obscured and there is a slight chill in the air.

A fakir has come to the door, there is a parrot on his hand. There is no cage, but it seems the parrot has forgotten how to fly. On their arrival it is the parrot that speaks, not the fakir: "Rama! Rama! Chant the name Rama, chant the name Rama!"

I said, "The parrot speaks well!"

The fakir said, "Sir, this parrot is a great *pundit*!"

On hearing this I laughed. I said, "It must be so, because all pundits are nothing but parrots."

I see it very clearly, that knowledge is not attained through learning, and what is attained through learning is not knowledge. Knowledge is not an achievement of the intellect. The intellect is only a memory system, and knowledge is not attained through memory, but through discarding memory. What comes through learning makes one only a parrot. This parrot-talk is called learnedness. There is no bigger obstacle than this on the path of knowledge.

Scholarship is an accumulation of dead facts. All these facts are borrowed ones, they do not have any roots in experience. A mind covered with these dead facts is unable to see that which *is*. These facts become a curtain.

The unknown is revealed as this curtain is removed.

This seeing is knowledge.

Seeing, not learning, is knowledge.

Seeing the truth – not the scriptures, not facts – is the way to attainment. When the truth is seen, one finds that the knowledge was already there, only we had no eyes to see it. And the eyes could not have been attained through an accumulation of scholarship. At the most, that could have created a self-deception, nothing else. Without really knowing, one could have derived ego-fulfillment – that one knows. This is why it is said that to know that "I know" is ignorance. Why? – because upon knowing, it is found that "I am not", only knowing *is;* neither the knower is there, nor the known.

This seeing of the non-dual happens when, discarding everything, I become empty.

ONE IS NOT TO SUPPRESS THE BODY

THE DUSK HAS DESCENDED and the fragrance of the evening flowers has begun to spread. A cuckoo has been calling the whole afternoon and now she has become quiet. When she was singing, she was not so much in my attention, but now becoming quiet she has entered my attention. I am waiting for her to call again, when a monk arrives. He is a celibate with a withered, lean and sickly body. His face is pallid and dull, his eyes are parched and dry. Seeing him I feel pity; he has ill-treated his body. I say this to him and he is almost shocked. He believes this to be the only renunciation – as if ill-health is spiritual, as if ugliness and disfiguration is yoga practice, as if disciplining something repulsive is the spiritual discipline.

Count Keyserlingk has written somewhere, "Health is an anti-spiritual ideal." In this there is an echo of the same ignorance. This thought is born out of reaction. There are people who are interested only in the body; the physical body is all for them, this is one extreme; then as a reaction to this the other extreme is born – but both the extremes are materialistic.

Neither has one to go on indulging one's body all over the place, nor has one to go on crippling it. On the whole it is but a dwelling. It is essential that it is healthy and well.

Spiritual life is not antagonistic to health. In fact, it is total health. It is synonymous with a state of harmonious and melodious beauty.

Suppression of the body is not spirituality; it is only hedonism doing a headstand. It is only a reaction to a life of indulgence. There is no knowledge in it, only ignorance and self-torture. It is a violent tendency. No one reaches anywhere through it. One is not to suppress the body; it is only an innocent instrument and a follower. It adapts to wherever I am: in desires and passions, it keeps me company there. If I move into spiritual discipline, it be-comes a companion there, it follows me. Transformation is not to be wrought in it, but in the one whom it follows.

I AM TALKING OF PEACE, bliss and liberation. This alone is the central quest of life. If it is not realized, life is wasted. Yesterday I was saying this when a young man asked, "Can everybody attain liberation? And if everybody can, why then is it not simply attained?" I told him a story....

One morning, someone had asked this same question to Gautam Buddha. Buddha had asked him to go round the city, and come back after inquiring who wants what in life. The man went from door to door and returned by the evening utterly exhausted, but with a complete list. Somebody wanted fame, somebody wanted position, somebody wanted health, prosperity and affluence, but not a single person had wanted liberation. Buddha said, "Tell me now – now ask me the question! Everybody can attain liberation. It is already there, but can you at least look at it even once? We are standing with our backs turned to it."

This is my answer too. Everybody can attain liberation, just as every seed can become a plant. It is our potential, our possibility, but this potential has to be turned into actuality. This much I know – the act of a seed turning into a plant is not difficult. It is very easy. The seed has only to be ready to die and the sprout comes out at the same moment. If I am ready to die, liberation comes instantly.

The 'I' is the bondage: as it goes, liberation is. With the 'I', I am in the world; without the 'I', I myself am the liberation.

94 ONE HAS TO BECOME WHOLE

A YEAR HAS PASSED. During the last rainy season I sowed the seeds of *gultevari* flowers. When the rainy season was over, the flowers also disappeared. Then I removed the dried-up plants. This year I am seeing that with the coming of the rains so many *gultevari* plants are sprouting on their own. They have begun to appear from the ground in so many places. The seeds left in the ground from the previous season have waited for a year, and are blissfully coming to life now. In the darkness underground, in winter and summer, they have been waiting there. Now somehow they have the opportunity to see the light again. With this comes the feeling of an auspicious and festive music emanating from those newly born plants, and I experience it.

Centuries ago, some nectar-sweet-throat sang: *Tamaso ma jyotirga-maya* – lead me from darkness to light. Who does not have the desire to move from darkness to light!

Are not such seeds lying hidden in every man, in every living being, wanting to attain to light? Is there not also for many, many lifetimes, a waiting and praying for this opportunity?

These seeds are lying hidden within everyone, and it is only from these seeds that the thirst arises for becoming complete. These flames are lying hidden in everyone, and these flames want to reach out to the sun! No one becomes fulfilled without transforming these seeds into plants. There is no other way than to become whole. One has to become whole, because intrinsically every seed is whole.

95 LET THE KNOWN GO

ANEW MORNING.

A new sun.

A new sunshine.

New flowers.

I have just woken up. Everything is new and fresh; there is nothing old and stale in existence.

Many hundreds of years ago Heraclitus in Greece said, "It is impossible to step into the same river twice."

Everything is new, but man becomes outdated. Man simply does not live in the new, hence he becomes outdated. Man lives in memory, in the past, in the dead. This is mere living, but not life. This is half-death, and taking this half-death for life, one day we pass away. Life is neither in the past nor in the future. Life is ever in the present.

That life is attained through yoga, because yoga makes one awake into everlasting freshness. It makes one wake up into the eternal now. Yoga makes one wake up into the eternal present.

One has to wake up into that which is. What was is no more, what will be is not yet, and what is is revealed only when man's mind is free from the burden of memory and imagination. Memory is an accumulation of the dead past; life cannot be attained through it. Imagination also is only the offshoot of memory, it is only its echo and projection. All this is only wandering about in the known. The doors of the unknown do not open through it.

Let the known go, so that the unknown may manifest.

Let the dead go so that the living may manifest.

This alone is the essence of yoga.

THE NIGHT IS DEEPENING. There are only a few stars in the sky and a not-yet-full moon is hanging in the west. The jasmine has blossomed, and its fragrance is floating in the air.

I have just seen a lady to the door and returned. I do not know her. Some suffering has engulfed her mind, its darkness has formed an aura all around her. I felt this aura of suffering as she came in. Without wasting time, she asked me at once, "Can suffering be destroyed?" I looked at her. She appeared to be a living monument to suffering.

Slowly, slowly, people are all becoming such monuments. They all want to destroy suffering but are unable to do so, because their diagnosis of suffering is not correct. Suffering exists in a certain state of consciousness; it is the characteristic feature of that state. Within that state there is no freedom from suffering, because that state itself *is* the suffering. In it, if you remove one sorrow, another takes its place; this chain continues. You may free yourself from this sorrow or that sorrow, but freedom from suffering as such does not happen. The suffering remains, only the causes change.

The elimination of suffering, the freedom from suffering happens in changing the state of consciousness, not in becoming free of individual sorrow.

On a dark night a young man approached Gautam Buddha. He was sad, worried and anguished. He said, "What a suffering the world is! What a torment it is!" Gautam Buddha said, "Come to where I am – there is no suffering here, there is no anguish here."

There is a state of consciousness in which there is no suffering. It was to indicate towards this consciousness that Buddha had used the term: "where I am".

There are two states of human consciousness: one of ignorance, the other of knowing – one of identification with the other, and the second of self-realization. As long as I identify myself with the other, there is suffering. This bondage with the other is suffering. Becoming free from the other, realization of the self, being in the self, is the elimination of suffering. I am not yet I, hence the suffering. When I actually become I, suffering ceases.

97 THIS PARADOX IS THE LAW OF LIFE

TONIGHT THE SKY IS not studded with stars. It is overcast with dark clouds which drizzle now and then. The flowers of the nightqueen have bloomed, filling the winds with their fragrance.

I am almost as though I am not. And in this not being, the being has become.

There is a world where death is life, and where to be lost is to find. Once I used to think that the drop is to be submerged into the ocean; now I find that the ocean itself has fallen into the drop.

For man, to 'be' is his bondage, to be empty is his liberation. This tension of 'being' makes one wander off unnecessarily. And the fear of becoming empty stops one from becoming the whole. As long as there is no readiness to become nothing, one remains nothing. As long as there is no courage to move into death, one has to move around in death. But the one who becomes ready to receive death finds that there *is* no death, and the one who becomes ready to be annihilated finds that there is something in him which cannot be annihilated.

This paradox is the law of life. To know this law is yoga, and to know it well is to be free. It is the ignorance of this law that makes one wander off. By knowing it, all our wandering ceases, and that which is attained is the end of the journey, not just an overnight stay.

98 DESIRE, BY ITS NATURE, IS INSATIABLE

ONE FULL-MOON NIGHT, a few people from the pub went to the river for boating. They rowed continuously from midnight to dawn. When the cold morning wind blew and the sun rose, their drunkenness began to fade. They thought it was time to return, and they came down on the bank to see how far they had traveled. But there was no end to their amazement when they discovered that the boat stood exactly where they had found it the previous night! In the night they had quite forgotten that only rowing the boat was not enough; the boat needs to be untied also.

I told this tale in the evening. An old gentleman had come to see me. He said, "I have been walking my whole life, but now at the end, it feels as if I have not reached anywhere." It is to him I had to tell this story.

Man is not conscious. Ignorance of his self is his unconsciousness. In this unconsciousness all his actions are mechanical. He moves in this unintelligent state as if in sleep and he reaches nowhere. Just as the chains of that boat remained tied to some post on the bank, in this state he too remains tied somewhere.

Religion has called this bondage desire. Man, tied to his desires, remains under the delusion of coming closer and closer to bliss, but one day this whole hurry proves to be a mirage. No matter how much he rows, his boat will just not leave the shore of unfulfillment. He leaves life empty and unfulfilled.

Desire, by its nature, is insatiable. Life runs out, and the life in which the other shore could have been attained – the life in which the journey could have been completed – is wasted, and it is discovered that the boat has not moved at all.

Every sailor knows that before launching the boat into the ocean it has to be untied from the shore. Every man should also know that before launching his life's boat into the ocean of bliss, fulfillment and light, the chains of desire have to be disconnected from the shore. After that, perhaps even rowing is not needed.

Ramakrishna has said, "You take up the anchor, you set the sails; the winds of the divine are eager to carry you each moment."

99 BLISS IS THE CENTER

A HERMIT CAME to me yesterday. We talked about the discipline of meditation. It is very surprising to hear the mistaken and false ideas that prevail regarding the nature of mind. If we begin the discipline with the assumption that the mind is our enemy, the entire discipline goes wrong. Neither is the mind our enemy, nor the body. They are mere instruments and are helpful. Consciousness can use them just as it likes. The attitude of enmity and conflict creates suppression from the very onset, and as a result the whole of life gets poisoned.

The human mind, by its very nature, is inclined to bliss and there is nothing wrong in it. It is nothing but its attraction towards self-nature. If bliss were not there, man could never move toward the spiritual life. The mind seeks for bliss first in the world, and when it does not find it there, it turns inwards.

Bliss is the center – both of the world and of liberation. It is on the axis of this bliss that the whole worldly and the other-worldly life revolves.

The glimpse of bliss is seen on the outside; hence the race outside. Through meditation the real source of this bliss becomes visible, so the direction turns towards the source.

But the mind is not to be forcibly turned inwards. It is because of suppression that mind starts appearing like an enemy.

No, a new dimension of bliss is to be opened. As soon as that dimension is opened, the mind is found to be moving withinwards on its own. Its inclination is towards bliss, and where there is bliss, it has a natural movement towards it.

Bliss is the goal of life. Bliss, unending bliss, is the purpose of life. In the world come the glimpses, the reflection: its original source is in liberation. Outside is its projection, inside the roots. On the circumference is its shadow, in the center its life. Hence, the world is not in contradiction to liberation; the outside is not the enemy of the inside. The whole existence is a symphony.

The moment this truth is seen, man falls out of bondage.

100 GIVE UP ALL CONCEPTS AND THEN SEE

IN THE EARLY MORNING HOURS a young man came. He looked sad, and it seemed as if some loneliness was enveloping him from within, as if he had lost something and his eyes seemed to be searching for it. He has been visiting me for nearly a year now, and this too I knew well, that one day he would come like this. Before this, there was an imaginary bliss in him which has now gradually disappeared.

For a while there was silence. The young man closed his eyes and seemed to be thinking about something. Then he spoke openly: "I have lost my trust. I lived in dreams, which have been shattered now. I used to feel God to be with me; now I am left alone and I feel puzzled. Never before was I so helpless. I want to go back, but that too does not seem possible now. That bridge is ruined."

I tell him that only that which was not, can be taken away. It is not possible to take away that which is. Loneliness only gets suppressed in the unconsciousness – not destroyed – through the companions of dream and imagination. The bliss attained through imagination and the mental projection of God is not real. It is a delusion, not a support. And the sooner one gets rid of delusions the better.

To really attain to God, one has to renounce all mental concepts – and the concept of God is not an exception; that too has to be renounced. This is the only renunciation and this is the only asceticism, because there is no greater hardship than renouncing dreams.

At the point of disappearance of imagination, dreams and concepts, that which is manifests; sleep shatters and wakefulness comes. Then the attainment is the real attainment, because nobody can take it away. And it is not disrupted by any other experience, because it is one's own experience, not an experience of others. It is not the seeing of any scene, it is a realization of the pure seer himself. It is not a thought about God, it is being in God.

Do not panic if the imaginary concept of God and trust in God have disappeared. This can only be good. Give up all concepts and then see.

What is seen then *is* God.

A FRIEND HAS PRESENTED some paper flowers to me. I look at these flowers – there is nothing in them beyond that which is visible to the eyes. Everything in them is visible, there is nothing of the invisible. Outside in the flowerbeds roses are in bloom, and beyond the visible there is something of the invisible in them, and this invisible dimension is their very breath itself.

Modern civilization is analogous to paper flowers. It ends at the visible, with the seen, and hence is lifeless. It has lost its link with the unknown, the invisible. And this is why man is so cut off, so separated from his own roots as never before.

The tree, its leaves, its flowers, its fruits are all visible, but the roots are under the earth. The roots are in the unknown and invisible. The roots that can be seen are not the end of all roots – there are other roots that cannot be seen. The center where life is linked with the universal life is not only unknown, but is also unknowable.

A man connected with the unknowable attains to the real roots.

The unknowable cannot be attained through thoughts. The limit of thought ends at the knowable and visible – thought itself is knowable and visible. And that which is visible cannot become the medium for knowing the invisible.

Is-ness is beyond thoughts, existence is transcendental to thoughts.

Hence, one does not *know* existence, rather one *becomes* existence. One is not to become acquainted with it as an onlooker, separate from it; rather, one has to become one with it.

Dropping thoughts, becoming calm and empty, so comes that non-duality which puts one into truth, into is-ness. If one has to see paper flowers, if they can be seen from a distance, one can become a seer to them. If the real flowers are to be seen, one has to become the flower.

102 WHAT IS MATURITY?

A GIRL IS CRYING; her doll is broken. And now I think: is not all our weeping a weeping over broken dolls?

Last evening an old man came to see me. What he had wished for in his life could not happen. He was sad and sorrowful. Today I met a lady who every now and then wiped her tears as she talked to me: she had dreams and they did not come true.

And now, this girl is weeping. Is there not a basic reflection of all tears in the tears of this girl? Has not the root cause of all tears taken form in the broken doll lying in front of her? Somebody is consoling her, that after all it is only a toy, and what is there to weep for? Hearing it, I could not help laughing. If man were to realize this truth, would not all his sorrows come to an end? How difficult it is to understand that a doll is merely a doll!

Man hardly matures to the extent that he can understand this. The maturing of man's body is one thing, man himself maturing is quite another. What is maturity?

Man's maturity is in becoming free of the mind. As long as the mind is there it goes on creating toys. Freedom from toys happens as soon as one is free of the mind.

103 NOT TO DO ANYTHING IS MEDITATION

"I AM A SEEKER. I am engaged in spiritual disciplines and I am making progress. One day the attainment is also going to happen." – once a hermit said this to me. In his words I felt more the ring of desire than of spiritual discipline. Such spiritual disciplines are themselves obstacles.

What is there to practice to attain that which already is? It is not even to be attained – only to recognize that it has never been lost. And the whole undertaking of the so-called spiritual practice hides this truth. At the root of this is one's sensual desire, and a wish to attain something, to change something: I am to change from what I am, **A** is to be changed into **B**. This duality, this conflict, lies at the root of all sensual desires. This duality is the world and sorrow.

I say: if you desire to be even slightly different from what you are, you are going against what is. And what is, is the path. The moment one wakes up to what is, one's life is filled with a naturalness and beauty; a freedom and liberation permeates one's every breath. This beauty is never available to the so-called practitioner. A violence, a suppression and a kind of lust for becoming destroys that naturalness. Hence, there is an ugliness found in all the so-called aspiring ascetics.

Then what shall we do? Nothing. Not to do, not to do anything, is meditation. The self is neither in doing nor in thoughts. It is discovered the moment actions and thoughts are dispelled.

Drop everything, let go of everything, let everything disappear. And then what is seen in this nothingness, in this emptiness, is everything.

THERE IS A PARABLE:

Once a youth asked a hermit, "What is the method to attain liberation?" The hermit replied, "Who has bound you?" The youth paused for a moment and then said, "Nobody has bound me."

Then the hermit asked, "Then why do you search for liberation?"

Why do you search for liberation? – this is what I also asked one person yesterday. This is what every person has to ask himself: where is the bondage?

Wake up to what *is*! Stop bothering about changing that which is – don't run after ideals. You are what is in the present, not what is in the future. And there is no bondage in the present. The moment one wakes up to the present, bondages are not found anywhere.

Desire...in the very desire to become something and attain something is the bondage. A desire is always in the future, always in the tomorrow. And that is the bondage, that is the tension, that is the race, that is the world. It is the desire itself that creates the idea of liberation. And if bondage is at the roots, how can liberation be the outcome?

The beginning of liberation has to be in freedom. Liberation is not just the end, it is the beginning as well.

It is not that liberation has to be attained; rather it has to be seen that "I am already in a state of liberation." The realization that "I am liberated" is attained effortlessly in a calm, wakeful consciousness. Everybody is already liberated: it is only a matter of waking up to this reality.

The moment I drop all going, the moment the race for becoming something goes away, I fully become. And this 'becoming', in its full sense, *is* liberation.

The so-called religious person does not attain to this becoming because he is in a race for attaining liberation, for attaining the soul, for attaining to God. And the one who is in a race, whatever the form of that race, is not in himself. To be religious is not a matter of faith, of effort or of doing. To be religious is a matter of being in oneself. And this liberation can come in a moment.

The moment one becomes aware of the truth that bondage is in desiring, in racing, in ideals, the darkness disappears and no bondage is found in what is then seen.

Truth brings revolution in a moment.

IT IS A WINTER MORNING, the sun has just risen. There were cold winds in the night, and earlier in the morning the grass was covered with dewdrops. Now the rays have absorbed them, and the sunlight has become warmer.

A pleasant morning has heralded the day. How meaningful even the meaningless songs of birds seem to be! But perhaps life has no meaning, and the imagination of meaning is man's own idea. There is no meaning – perhaps that is why there is infinite depth and vastness in life. Meaning is a limitation.

Life, existence, is limitless; hence there is no meaning in it at all. He who makes himself limitless by his merger with the meaningless, he who becomes meaningless in this vast meaninglessness, attains to that which is, attains to existence.

All meaning is petty and is of the petty. All meaning has been given by the ego. Ego is the center of all these meanings. The world that is seen through it is not the real world. Whatsoever is related to 'I' is not real.

Truth is an indivisible whole: it is not divided into 'I' and 'not-I'. All meaning is from the 'I'; hence the indivisible, the one which is beyond 'I' and 'not-I', is without meaning – it has neither meaning nor no-meaning. It is wrong to give it any name. Even to call it God is wrong! God too is in reference to the I, God too is a concept of the I.

Let us say that whatever is meaningful is really meaningless. To go beyond the limit of meaningfulness is to become spiritual.

Someone asked Bodhidharma, "Please say something about the sacred nirvana." Bodhidharma replied, "There is nothing sacred in it, just emptiness and only emptiness."

106 IN THIS WORDLESS CONSCIOUSNESS

A COCK IS CROWING.... I listen.

A cart is passing on the path.... I watch.

There is hearing, there is seeing, but no word in between. Words separate one from existence. Words are *about* the truth, they are not themselves the truth. One reaches the truth by dropping words, not through them. And to be wordless is samadhi, enlightenment.

But being wordless alone is not samadhi: words are absent in unconsciousness and in sleep too. Being wordless and yet remaining wakeful, conscious and alert is samadhi.

I am saying this to a hermit. He believes absorption and unconsciousness of the senses to be samadhi. Many have carried this fallacy; this fallacy is very dangerous. It is because of this fallacy that worship, devotion and many such methods of becoming unconscious have become prevalent. All these methods are nothing but escapes, and their utility is nothing different from that of intoxicants. In them, a person forgets himself. Due to this forgetfulness, due to this self-forgetfulness, an illusion of bliss is created. But meditation requires complete self-remembrance, not self-forgetfulness. When one is fully awake, one *is*.

I am completely in my self. This awakening happens from becoming free of words, thoughts and the mind. In this wordless consciousness the 'I' disappears. But I do not disappear; rather, on disappearance of the 'I', on disappearance of the sense of ego, I become fully myself.

107 RECOLLECT YOUR OWN DIVINITY

THE DARK NO-MOON NIGHT is descending. The birds have returned to their nests, and in the gathering darkness there is great chirping on the trees before they retire. The lamps are being lit in the city. In a short while, the sky is going to be studded with stars and the earth glittering with lamps.

Two tiny dark patches of clouds are floating in the eastern sky. There is no companion with me – I am all alone. There is no thought, I am just sitting. How blissful it is just to sit! The sky and the galaxy of stars seem to have submerged me.

When there are no thoughts, the individual existence merges with the universal existence. There is only a small curtain; otherwise everybody is the existence himself.

There is a thin veil on our eyes, and it is hiding existence. This thin veil itself has become the world. The moment this cover is removed the doors to the kingdom of infinite bliss are thrown open.

Jesus Christ has said, "Knock and the doors shall be opened." I say: Just take a look – the doors are already open.

One man was running towards the setting sun. He asked another man, "Where is the east?" The reply came, "You just turn around and you will have the east right before your eyes."

All is present – what one needs is to turn one's eyes in the right direction.

This statement has to be declared to the whole world! Even to have rightly listened to it is to have attained much. The trust in the divinity of oneself is half the attainment.

Just today I said to a friend who had come to see me, "The treasure is already within you, you have simply forgotten about it. Awaken the right-remembrance, recollect your own divinity, know who you are. Ask yourself – and ask yourself to the extent that only this inquiry remains, resounding through your entire mind and being. Then its arrow moves directly to your unconscious, and a mystical response comes right in front of you of its own accord, which to know, is to know everything."

108 IN UTTER ALONENESS

THE NIGHT HAS NOT YET given way to the dawn, and the sky is still studded with departing stars. The river looks like a thin stream of silver. The sand is cool with dewdrops, and the wind is bitter with cold. A deep stillness prevails, and the sounds of birds every now and then only deepens it.

Taking a friend with me, I have come to this solitary place rather early. The friend says that he feels fear in solitude, and the stillness feels overwhelming. If he keeps himself occupied somehow then it is fine; otherwise a strange kind of anguish and sadness overtakes him.

This anguish comes to everybody. Nobody wants to face himself. Looking within oneself, one feels puzzled. And because solitude leaves one alone with oneself, it is frightening. If you are entangled in the other, the self is forgotten. That is a kind of unconsciousness and an escape. Man keeps himself busy his whole life in this escape.

But this escape is temporary: there is no way man can escape from his own self! All his efforts to escape are futile, because he himself is the one from whom he is trying to escape. How can one escape from oneself, and how can one run away from oneself? We can run away from everything, but not from our own self. Having run throughout our whole life, we will find that we have not reached anywhere. Hence, those who are intelligent do not run away from their own self; rather, they face themselves.

If man looks inwards he experiences an emptiness. There is an infinite nothingness within. Hence, becoming puzzled, he runs outwards. He makes endless efforts to fill this emptiness. He wants to fill it up in the world, in relationships. But it cannot be filled in any way – it is impossible to fill it up – and this is his anguish and the failure of his life. Death shows this anguish very clearly: death throws him into this very emptiness from which he has been escaping his whole life. And that is why the fear of death is uppermost.

I say, fleeing from one's emptiness is ignorance. It is through facing it, entering it, that life is attained. Reaching to this nothingness, we realize our nature.

Religion is an entry into the emptiness. What man experiences in himself in utter aloneness is religiousness.

109 LIFE IS JUST FOR LIVING

"WHAT IS THE IDEAL of life?" a young man has asked.

The night has deepened and the sky is full of stars. The wind is cold, somebody said there had been a hailstorm in the region. The path is desolate and there is dense darkness under the trees.

How blissful it is to live in this calm, solitary night. Just to be is such bliss! But we have forgotten how to be.

How blissful this life is! But we do not want to just live, we want to live for some ideal. We want to turn life – which is the end in itself – into a means. This race for ideals poisons everything. This tension about ideals disrupts all the music of life.

Once Akbar asked Tansen, "How is it that you do not sing so well as your master does? There is some divinity of the beyond in his singing." Tansen replied, "My master sings only for the sake of singing, while I sing for some purpose."

Some time try *just* living. Just live – do not struggle with life, do not force life. Quietly watch things happening. Let what happens happen. Allow that which is to just be. Drop all tensions from your side and let life flow, let life happen. And what will happen, I assure you, liberates.

The illusion of ideals is one of the blind faiths cherished through the ages. Life is just for living – not for someone else, not for something else. One who lives for some reason does not really live. One who just lives, *really* lives…and he alone attains to that which is worth attaining. It is also he who attains to the ideal.

I look at the young man. An amazing peace has descended on his face. He does not say a word, but he says everything. He goes after sitting silently and peacefully for an hour, a transformed man. He says at the time of his leaving, "I go from here a different person."

110 RELATIONSHIPS ARE NOT OBSTACLES

IT IS MORNING. The sun is behind the clouds and it is drizzling. The rain has created a humidity all around. A hermit, soaking wet, has come to see me. Some fifteen or twenty years back he had renounced his home to attain self-realization. The renunciation took place, but the attainment did not happen. Because of this he is sad. Society and relationships are considered obstacles in the way of self-attainment. Such a belief has unnecessarily cut people off from life.

I told him a story:

There was a mad woman. She was fully convinced that her body was not physical and that she had a divine body. She used to say that there was no other body on the earth more beautiful than her body. One day she was brought face to face with a full length mirror. She saw her body in the mirror and she was enraged. She threw a chair at the mirror and the mirror broke into pieces: she breathed a sigh of relief. When she was asked about the reason for breaking the mirror she said, "The mirror makes my body look physical. It distorts my beauty."

Society and relationships are no more than mirrors: they only reflect what is within you. As meaningless as it is to break a mirror, so it is to renounce relationships. It is the self, not the mirror, that is to be transformed. And this transformation can take place exactly where one is. This revolution begins from the center. To work on the periphery is to waste time unnecessarily.

One has to start work on the self directly.

Society and relationships are not obstacles in any way.

Obstacles, if any, are in oneself.

111 A BASE IN THE INNER SELF

"IS THERE A GOD?" We don't know.

"Is there a soul?" We don't know.

"Is there life after death?" We don't know.

"Is there a meaning in life?" We don't know.

"We don't know" is the whole philosophy of life today. In these three words is contained our whole knowledge. There is no end to our race as far as knowing about matter, about the other is concerned, but about the self, about consciousness, we go on drowning in more and more darkness every day.

The outside seems to be in light, but the inside is in pitch darkness. There is knowledge on the circumference and ignorance at the center. And the surprising thing is that not even an effort is needed to illumine the center. Just as your vision falls there, all is illuminated. We have only to turn our eye inside and see everything there illumined.

If our eye is not on the other, it opens upon the self. If it has no base available on the outside, it finds a base in the inner self.

Self-based consciousness is samadhi, enlightenment.

Samadhi is the door to truth.

In it one does not find the answer; rather, all the questions drop.

And the disappearing of all questions is the real answer. Where there are no questions but only consciousness, pure consciousness, there is the answer, the knowing.

Without attaining this knowing, life is a sheer waste.

112 THE BODY-MIND IS AN INN

ONE NIGHT A TRAVELER was staying at an inn. When he arrived there a few other travelers were just departing. Next morning when he was ready to depart, he saw some other travelers checking in. The guests at the inn would come and go, but the host always remained there. A hermit saw this and asked if the same phenomenon was not happening with man every day.

I also ask the same, and say that there is nothing greater in life than recognizing the guest and the host.

The body-mind is an inn: the guests of thoughts, feelings and desires are visiting it. But something separate from the guests is also there – the host is also there. But who is this host? How to know this host?

Buddha has said, "Stop!" – and this stopping itself is knowing it.

Buddha's full statement is: "This mad mind does not stop. If it can stop, that itself is enlightenment, that itself is nirvana."

As the mind stops, the host reveals himself. It is pure, eternal, wakeful consciousness. It is never born, it never dies. Neither is it bound nor is it liberated. It only is…and its is-ness is supreme bliss.

113 CONSOLING ONESELF WITH TALES

L IFE – WHAT WE UNDERSTAND as life – what is it? Last night somebody put this question to me. I told him a story:

Once a young man and an old man were sitting on easy chairs in a waiting room. The old man had his eyes shut, but he would smile from time to time. And sometimes he would make gestures with his hands and face, as if he was trying to keep something away from himself.

The young man could not help asking him, "What is it about this ugly waiting room which makes you smile?" The old man said, " I am telling stories to myself, and some of these make me laugh."

The young man then asked, "And what is it which you try to keep away with gestures of your hands and face?" The old man started laughing and he said, "It is those stories which I have heard too many times."

The young man said, "What to say? You are consoling yourself with stories!" In reply the old man said, "My son, one day you will understand that the whole of life is nothing but consoling oneself with stories."

Certainly, life as we know it is nothing but a tale – and to console oneself with tales is what our life is. What we understand as life is not life, but a dream. It is on waking up that we realize that our hands were empty with what was not really there; it only appeared to be there.

But it is possible to awaken from this dream-life to the real life. The sleep can be dropped, the one who is sleeping can wake up. In the very possibility of sleeping is also the possibility to awaken.

114 AWAKEN TO YOUR OWN TRUTH

IT IS ABOUT MIDNIGHT. After many days, the sky is clear today. Everything looks freshly showered and the half-moon is sinking into the western horizon.

This evening I spoke at the prison. There were many prisoners present. How simple they become, what a purity starts emanating from their eyes as one talks to them – all this is coming to my memory.

There, I said: there is no sinner in the eyes of God, just as there is no darkness in the presence of light. Hence, I do not ask you to drop anything. I do not ask you to drop the dirt, I only ask you to attain the diamonds. You attain the diamonds and the dirt drops away on its own accord. Those who ask you to renounce something are stupid: the world exists solely for the purpose of attainment. When one attains a new rung of the ladder, the previous one is renounced on its own. Renunciation is negative: it has pain, sorrow and suppression in it. Attainment is positive: it has bliss in it. The act of renunciation appears to be the first step, but in fact it is attainment that comes first. Before the first rung is renounced, the second rung has already been attained. It is only after attaining it, after realizing that it has been attained, that the first rung is renounced. Hence, if you attain to the divine, then what appears like sin goes away without any effort on your part.

Indeed, in attaining that one, all is attained. The moment that truth comes to us, all dreams disappear on their own accord. Dreams are not to be renounced, but to be known. One who engages himself in renouncing the dreams has already accepted their reality. We don't believe in their reality. This is why we can say, "*Aham Brahmasmi* – I am Brahman." For those who proclaimed this, darkness has no existence whatsoever.

Friends, know this! Awaken the light within yourself and call out. Experience the divine within yourself. Awaken to your own truth, and then it is found that darkness is nowhere. Our own unconsciousness is darkness, our own awakening becomes the light.

I said this to those prisoners, but then I felt this has to be said to everyone, because is there anyone who is not a prisoner?

115 EVERYBODY IS TALKING TO HIMSELF

TODAY I WAS PRESENT in a seminar. I was present, but my presence was almost like a non-presence. I was not a participant, I was only an audience. What I heard there was ordinary, but what I saw there was certainly extraordinary.

There was argumentation on every single idea. I heard it all, but what came to light was something else. I saw that the argumentation was about the 'I', not about the ideas and issues. Nobody was interested in proving anything but his own 'I'.

The basic root of all discussions is in the 'I'. No matter where its center may appear to be on the surface, indirectly it is always there in the 'I'.

Roots are always indirect, they are invisible. What is visible is not the root; what is visible as flowers and leaves is secondary. If one stops at the visible there is no solution, because the problem itself is not there. The solution is at the same place where the problem is. Discussions reach nowhere, and the reason is, that we don't even pay any attention to seeing where the roots are.

This too can be seen: that where there is a discussion, nobody in fact speaks to the other, everybody talks to himself. It only appears that some talk is going on. But where there is 'I' there is a wall which makes it difficult to reach the other. It is impossible to have a dialogue while carrying one's 'I' with oneself.

Most of the people in the world thus spend their lives in talking to themselves.

I have read about an incident in a lunatic asylum. Two lunatics were engaged in a conversation. Their doctor was surprised to observe one thing – that they certainly were having a dialogue. While one would speak, the other would remain silent, but there was no connection, no relevance between what the two said. He asked them, "When you have only to babble your things, how is it that one of you remains silent when the other speaks?" They said, "We know the rules of conversation: while one speaks it is necessary for the other to remain silent – according to the rules."

This statement is very true – and true not only about lunatics, but about everybody. We observe the rules of conversation, but still everybody is talking to himself.

Without dropping the 'I' there is no way of communicating with the other. And the 'I' disappears only in love, hence, dialogue happens only in love. Other than that, everything is argumentation – and argumentation is insanity, because in it everything is being said by oneself to oneself.

When I was leaving from that seminar someone said to me, "Sir, you did not speak." I replied, "Nobody has spoken here."

116 THE PARTICIPANT WAS JUST A PROJECTION

I JUST AWAKENED FROM a dream. On awakening, one truth was seen: in the dream I was a participant as well as a watcher. As long as I had been in the dream the watcher was forgotten, only the participant remained. Now that I am awake I see that only the watcher was there, the participant was just a projection.

The dream and the world are both alike. The watcher, the consciousness alone, is the truth; all else is imaginary. What we have

known as 'I' is not real; only the one who knows this 'I' is real.

The watcher of everything is independent of all and is beyond all. Neither has it ever done anything, nor has anything happened to it – it only is.

When the unreal 'I' – the dream 'I' – ceases to exist, then that which is manifests. To realize this is liberation.

117 ATTAIN THE TRUE CENTER

A HERMIT ONCE TOLD ME, "I have renounced everything for God and now I have nothing left."

I see that truly he has nothing left, but I tell him that he still possesses that which he should have renounced, that which is the only thing that could have been renounced.

He looks all around. He really has no possessions: what he has is inside him. It is in his eyes, it is in his renunciation, it is in his sannyas… it is his 'I'. To renounce that is the only renunciation, for everything else can be taken away, and finally death takes away everything. It is only the 'I' which none can take away – not even death. It cannot be taken away: it can only be dropped, it can only be renounced. And the renunciation of that which cannot be taken away is the only real renunciation.

Hence, man has nothing but the 'I' which is worth offering to the divine. Every other renunciation is only an illusion, because that which he renounced did not belong to him in the first place. On the contrary, all the other renunciations only intensify and crystallize his ego. Even if one offers his life, from the center of 'I', it is no offering at all. Except for giving away the 'I', no other giving is a giving.

'I' is the only possession.

'I' is the only world. He alone who drops it is a non-possessor, a sannyasin. 'I' is the world; the absence of 'I' is sannyas.

To give away the 'I' is the real spiritual revolution and transformation, because it is in the space left empty by this 'I' where that arrives which is not *my* I, but that of the whole.

I love one statement of Simone Weil in which she says that only God has the right to call himself 'I'.

Indeed, only he who is the center of the whole existence has the right to call himself 'I'. But he has no reason to call himself 'I', because all and everything is 'I' for him. The one who has the right to do so has no reason; the one who has the reason to do so has no right.

But man can drop this no-right status and *can* attain the right. As he drops becoming the 'I' he can *be* I. Dropping the illusion of his center, he can attain the true center. The moment he dissolves his own center, he instantly attains to the center.

Man's 'I' is not real: it is a composite, it has no existence of its own; it is an accumulation. The illusion of truth that arises out of this accumulation is ignorance. But for one who looks into this accumulation and searches for the truth, the illusion is shattered and all the flowers in the garland of 'I' are scattered. Then that thread which is real is attained around which were strung the flowers of 'I', and which was covered by these flowers.

On removing these flowers, on shattering the cover formed by them, it is discovered that their base, the thread, is not only my base alone – it is in all, just as it is in me, and it passes through the whole of existence.

One who does not pass through this death of the 'I' remains deprived of the fulfillment of being a god. The death of the 'I' is the death of our distance and separation from God, from truth, from existence, as well as the distance that keeps us separate from ourselves. Blessed is the person who attains to this death before his physical death.

H E WHO LONGS for truth should know that he has not to accept any imagination, any concept of truth, because if he does, it is suicide to his spiritual endeavor.

In order to attain to truth one should have the courage to discard all temptations held out by the mind. None of the alternatives provided by the mind are to be accepted. Only then does a state beyond alternatives arise, which reveals one to oneself.

Before that blessed moment of direct and pure knowing becomes evident, one comes across much that is not the truth. And one who entangles himself in that will come to know everything but himself. The self is never known as an object of knowing. Hence, as long as there remains any trace of an object of knowing, know well that what you have encountered is 'the other', not the self. What remains when there is no object of knowing *is* the knowledge, *is* the self, *is* the truth.

Rinzai has said, "If on the path towards enlightenment you come across God himself, remove him from your path."

I also say the same: when the path to enlightenment is solitary, and when there is no object of knowing in the stream of knowledge, and when there remains nothing to be seen, only then is that which is the truth found and known.

Another master once said the same. One of his disciples heard this and went to his hut, broke all the statues and burnt all his scriptures. Then he returned to the master and said, "I have just destroyed all that is a hindrance to the arrival of the truth."

Hearing this, the master laughed and said, "You foolish boy! Burn those books that are inside you and break those idols which have become installed in your mind."

A similar thing happened here today. Inspired by my ideas, one young man destroyed his place of worship and threw his statues in a well before coming here. I told him, "Instead of throwing away the statues, throw away your mind which creates the statues. And to what avail is it to destroy the place of worship, as long as this mind is actively creating new places of worship and new images every moment?"

119 THE COURAGE TO BE ALONE

SOMEBODY WAS ASKING me about religion. I told him: religion has nothing to do with what you believe or do not believe. It is meaningful only if it becomes your breathing, not your faith. It is something which you either do or you do not do, which you either are or you are not. Religion is action, not mere talk.

Religion manifests in your actions only when it has become your essence first. Our actions become our being first. Before releasing the fragrance, it is essential to become a flower. Like the cultivation of flowers, the soul also needs to be cultivated.

And for the flowers to arise in the soul, it is not necessary to go to the mountains. They can be cultivated wherever you are, because you can be in the mountains while remaining exactly where you are. There are mountains and forests in the inner solitude of one's self.

This is so – truth and beauty are seen only in complete solitude. And whatever is great in life is attained by those who have the courage to be alone. The deeper secrets of life open their doors only in solitude, and the soul attains to love and light. Only when all is calm and quiet will those seeds sprout which are lying deep in the soil of our being, containing all our bliss in them. The growth happens from inside towards outside, and only in solitude. Remember, truth grows from inside. Artificial flowers can be imposed from outside, but as far as the real flowers are concerned, they grow from within.

For this inner growth it is not necessary to go to the outer mountains or forests, but it is necessary to be in that inner space. The path leading there is within everybody.

Take a few moments away from the hustle and bustle of your everyday rush, and forget the concepts of place and time around you, and your so-called personality, and the 'I' that is born out of it. Empty your mind of all that keeps it constantly full. Whatsoever comes to your mind, know well that you are not it and throw it out. Drop it all, everything – your name, your country, your family. Let all of it disappear from your memory and remain like a blank sheet of paper.

This very path is the path to our inner aloneness and solitude. It is through this that the inner sannyas finally happens.

When your mind drops all clinging, breaks all barriers of name and form, only then does that remain in you which is your real being.

In that moment you are alone, in solitariness.

What is known at that time is not of this world.

It is in this knowing that the flowers of religiousness bloom and life is filled with the fragrance of the divine.

What is known in these few moments – the silence, the beauty, the truth – gives you strength to live on two planes simultaneously. Then you are in the world, yet you are not of the world. Then there is no bondage, and life is liberated. You are in water, yet the water does not touch you.

In this very experience is the fulfillment of life, and the attainment of religiousness.

H E ALONE who has taken leave of all dogmas is on the path of truth. One who has some preferences, some dogmas to support – to him, truth cannot come. All preferences are the creation of man's mind. Truth is impartial. Hence, he who is unprejudiced, without a preference, becomes possessed by truth as well as its possessor.

So do not look for some preference, do not seek for some cult, do not seek some school of thought. Rather, let your mind reach the stage where all preferences are absent. It is only at that point that thoughts cease to exist, and 'seeing' begins. When the eyes become unprejudiced, *then* they are able to see that which is.

A truly religious person is he who has taken leave of all religions, who has no religion of his own. Thus dropping religions he becomes religious.

People ask me what religion I belong to. I answer, "I am religious, but I do not belong to any religion." That there can be many religions, I simply do not understand! Thoughts create differences. But it is not thoughts that lead one to religion; it is no-thought that leads one into religion – and there are no differences in no-thought.

Enlightenment is one, and the truth that is known in that state is also one. Truth is one, though doctrines are many. He who chooses one out of the diversity of doctrines, closes the doors against truth with his own hands. Set the doctrines free, and be free of them! Open the door for truth. This alone is my teaching.

East or West, the taste of the ocean is the same everywhere; the law of evaporation does not differ in different countries. The law of birth and death is the same for all: how then can our inner being be governed by different laws and truths?

There is no geography in the world of the soul; hence, there are no differences of direction and there are no borders. Differences, as such, originate in the mind, and he who is divided in the mind cannot attain to the indivisibility of the soul.

While returning from my morning walk I saw a bird in a cage. It reminded me of people imprisoned in prejudices. Prejudices are also cages, very subtle and self-created. We ourselves create them, nobody else – they are self-created prisons. First we create them; then becoming imprisoned in them we lose all capacity to fly in the open sky of truth.

And just now I see a kite flying in the sky. What freedom, what a liberation in its flight! One is a bird in a cage, the other a bird in flight in the open sky. Are not the two birds symbolic of two different states of our mind?

A bird flying in the sky does not leave any footprints, nor is any path created behind it. So it is with the sky of truth: those who are liberated fly in it, but neither are any footprints left behind, nor is any path created.

So remember that it is futile to search for any ready-made path towards truth. There is no such path. And it is good that it is so, because ready-made paths can lead you only to some kind of bondage – how can they liberate? Really, everybody has to create his own path to truth.

And how beautiful it is! Life is not like a train moving on rails: it is like a river running from beautiful mountains towards the ocean.

About the Author

Osho was born in Kuchwada, Madhya Pradesh, India, on December 11, 1931. From his earliest childhood, his was a rebellious and independent spirit, insisting on experiencing the truth for himself rather than acquiring knowledge and beliefs given by others.

After his enlightenment at the age of twenty-one, Osho completed his academic studies and spent several years teaching philosophy at the University of Jabalpur. Meanwhile, he traveled throughout India giving talks, challenging orthodox religious leaders in public debate, questioning traditional beliefs, and meeting people from all walks of life. He read extensively, everything he could find to broaden his understanding of the belief systems and psychology of contemporary man.

By the late 1960s Osho had begun to develop his unique Dynamic Meditation techniques. Modern man, he says, is so burdened with the outmoded traditions of the past and the anxieties of modern-day living that he must go through a deep cleansing process before he can hope to discover the thought-less, relaxed state of meditation.

In the course of his work, Osho has spoken on virtually every aspect of the development of human consciousness. He has distilled the essence of what is significant to the spiritual quest of contemporary man, based not on intellectual understanding but tested against his own existential experience.

He belongs to no tradition – "I am the beginning of a totally new religious consciousness," he says. "Please don't connect me with the past – it is not even worth remembering."

His talks to disciples and seekers from all over the world have been published in more than six hundred volumes, and translated into over thirty languages. And he says, "My message is not a doctrine, not a philosophy. My message is a certain alchemy, a science of transformation, so only those who are willing to die as they are and be born again into something so new that they cannot even imagine it right now...only those few courageous people will be ready to listen, because listening is going to be risky.

"Listening, you have taken the first step towards being reborn. So it is not a philosophy that you can just make an overcoat of and go bragging about. It is not a doctrine where you can find consolation for harassing questions. No, my message is not some verbal communication. It is far more risky. It is nothing less than death and rebirth."

Osho left his body on January 19, 1990. His huge commune in India continues to be the largest spiritual growth center in the world attracting thousands of international visitors who come to participate in its meditation, therapy, bodywork and creative programs, or just to experience being in a buddhafield.

OSHO COMMUNE INTERNATIONAL

The Osho Commune International in Poona, India, guided by the vision of the enlightened master Osho, might be described as a laboratory, an experiment in creating a 'new man' – a human being who lives in harmony with himself and his environment, and who is free from all ideologies and belief systems which now divide humanity.

The Osho Commune's Multiversity is the biggest and most comprehensive center for personal growth in the world today. It offers a wide variety of meditation and growth awareness programs, many of which are specifically designed for newcomers.

The eight faculties of the Multiversity cover all the healing arts of East and West, all the Western therapy approaches, the esoteric science, martial arts, creative arts and zen sports, a meditation academy and numerous trainings in many of these approaches.

All these programs are designed to help people to discover the knack of meditation: the passive witnessing of thoughts, emotions and actions, without judgment or identification.

Unlike many traditional Eastern disciplines, meditation at Osho Commune is an inseparable part of everyday life – working, relating or just being. The result is that people do not renounce the world but bring to it a spirit of awareness and celebration, in a deep reverence for life.

The highlight of the day at the Commune is the meeting of the Osho White Robe Brotherhood. This two-hour celebration of music, dance and silence, followed by a discourse from Osho, is unique – a complete meditation in itself where thousands of seekers, in Osho's words, "dissolve into a sea of consciousness."

SUGGESTED FURTHER READING

The following is a random selection from 450 book titles by Osho:

MEDITATION: THE FIRST AND LAST FREEDOM
A practical how-to guide, spotlighting over sixty meditation techniques – from Zazen, the ancient Buddhist practice of sitting, to Osho's cathartic Dynamic Meditation for the 21st-century seeker. In addition, Osho answers questions about the obstacles meditators may meet along the way.

THE SEARCH

TALKS ON THE TEN BULLS OF ZEN

The ten paintings that tell the Zen story about a farmer in search of his lost bull provide an allegorical expression of the inexpressible. Originally Taoist, they were repainted by the 12th century Chinese Zen master, Kakuan. Osho examines the deeper layers of meaning behind each painting, as well as answering questions from disciples and other seekers, in this special selection of discourses.

THE PSYCHOLOGY OF THE ESOTERIC

Osho travels beyond Freud and Jung, beyond the human potential movement, to enlightenment to buddhahood. He also talks on sex, love and prayer as the three essential steps to the divine. In addition He speaks on the significance of kundalini yoga, of dream psychology, of the seven energy bodies, and warns that 'esoteric games' can hinder growth.

NOWHERE TO GO BUT IN

In this Hindi translation, for the first time available in English, Osho talks on the nature of enlightenment, the seeking of spiritual powers, the relationship between meditation and love, love and marriage, meditation and sex, and sex as a meditation.

And in the last discourse, Osho talks of the spiritual heritage the Indians have received.

A CUP OF TEA

This book contains 365 letters that Osho wrote to disciples, friends and lovers while He was traveling in India from 1951 to the 1970s. A beautifully designed, gift size book.

I AM THE GATE

Osho speaks on the relationship between freedom and consciousness, defines His neo-sannyas, and elaborates on the mysteries of initiation and disciplehood.

THE GREAT CHALLENGE

This introduction to Osho's work includes the secret aspects of spiritual traditions, as well as talks on death, reincarnation and the scientific foundation of His revolutionary meditation technique, Dynamic Meditation.

THE GOOSE IS OUT

"This is the only ultimate joke in existence: you are enlightened, you are buddhas – pretending not to be, pretending to be somebody else. And my whole work here is to expose you."

Each question is an aspect of the human longing for freedom. And each answer flows to us from the peaks of total freedom, from the vision of enlightenment. Full of jokes and humor, irreverence, warmth and profound wisdom.

FOR FURTHER INFORMATION

To place an order or to make an inquiry about Osho's books, audio or video tapes, or for information about his meditations and an Osho meditation/information center near you, please contact:

Internet
http://www.osho.org

Osho Commune International
17 Koregaon Park
Pune 411 001 MS, India
Tel: +91 (0) 212 628 562, Fax: +91 (0) 212 624 181
e-mail: osho-commune@osho.org

Osho International
24 St. James's Street
London SW1A 1HA, UK
Tel: +44 (0) 171 925 1900, Fax: +44 (0) 171 925 1901
e-mail: osho_int@osho.org

Osho America
P.O. Box 2517, Scottsdale, AZ 85260, USA
Tel: +1 602 905 2612, Orders: +1 800 777 7743
Fax: +1 602 905 2618
e-mail: osho_america @osho.org